Tamar's Healing:

Out of the Darkness of Desolation into the Light of God's Glorious Love

By Reverend Kasim Ali Sidney Jones, Ed.D., M. Div.

Dr. Kasim Ali Sidney Jones

[handwritten inscription: To Cary / Peace, Power & Presence / Dr. Kasumu(?) ... / 10/29/2016]

This book is dedicated to Elizabeth Franklin, Cynthia Clark, Frances Jones, Arthur and Betty Calhoun, and Dorcas Devereux: Thank you for believing in me and inspiring me to keep moving.

Dr. Kasim Ali Sidney Jones

Acknowledgements

To God be the glory for all the things God has done.
There are not enough words in existence to express my
gratitude. Enough said... Amen!

To my family, especially Connie and Roy Anderson:
You had patiently and silently suffered as I gave of myself to
others and to this book. I do love and care for you more
than you will ever know. Shirley (Mom) and Tihira—two of
the three Shirleys: You have kept me grounded and focused,
even when you thought I could not hear you. You constantly
remind me why this book is necessary. I love you. To my
other brothers: Willie, Jr., Roy, Sr., and Duane; sisters-in-laws:
LaShondria, Shannon, Keisha; nieces: Pamela, LaShay,
Annamarie, Nakia, and Nicole; nephews: Roy, Jr and Montay;
aunts: Montra Bryant, Chistaunda Smith, Tahsa Bryant,
Cassie Ann, Almeeta Bryant, Annette Bryant,; uncles: Maurice
Bryant, Andrew Bryant, Willie Bryant, Jr. and the late Willie
Earl Bryant; and cousins: There are far too many of you to
begin listing, and I do not want to risk miss any of you: I am
you and you are me.

To my supportive friends: Keesha D. and Terry F.
Walker, Jr., David and Elijah Walker, Angellita S. Young,
Jeneice A. Richards, Kionna M. R. "BF" Richards, Arion D.
Knight, Alexandria Williams, Bruce Crandle, Audrey
"Melodie" and David McCray, Charlene Sims, Dawnya Ward,
Veronica and Johnnie Johnson, Gary L. Greene, and Miracle
Jefferson. Thank you all so very much for your presence and
support. I love you all.

To my church family the Chapel of Christian Love

Missionary Baptist Church (Atlanta, GA): As always, I thank you for embracing me and propping me up. To the children/youth and parents of the CCLBC: We make it happen when the Spirit of God is present. I love you all.

To American Bible University faculty, staff and students: God is doing so many wonderful things through this institution, and I count it a blessing to be in the midst. I thank you all for allowing to be a part of a powerful movement that is equipping and empowering God's servants for the work in God's kingdom.

To Glennisha S. White: My friend, my editor, my "sounding board," my mirror, my sister-friend... I am truly, truly blessed to have you in my life. You have inspired me to "Keep it moving" regardless of the situation, in spite of the distractions, and the hurdles that seem to pop up out of nowhere. Your support is a priceless asset in my life. God orders our steps, and causes us to experience many things, and to meet many people along the way. I count myself truly favored to have you as my friend. Thank you so much for sharing your wisdom, your insight, your in-depth suggestions and discussions, and most of all, your time. You are as much a part of this project as I am. I love you dearly, my friend.

To Tamar Grimes: You had a good laugh when you heard the title of this book—"Oh, I needed healing?" If I said you have been a good friend to me, it would be a great understatement. You have been a counselor when I really needed to hear what made logical sense put so plainly. "Come on now... it's not personal." I truly thank you for allowing cooler heads to prevail. I love you for holding that mirror up and saying, "This is you."

Dr. Kasim Ali Sidney Jones

To Lorice Austin: Accountability and boundaries. These are the things we have discussed in great detail. I thank you for holding my feet to the fire. I count you as a friend because you have done things that a friend does: Tell it like it is, no matter what. I thank you and I love you for everything.

To Doctor Olayinka Olubunmi "Best Sister" Williams and Doctor Dana L. "My PDS" Taylor: As always, thank you for inspiring me to do my best and keep writing as God would have me to. I love you.

To my Pastor and First Lady, Reverend Doctor James Allen, Sr. and Janice Hardaway Milner: Thank you for your prayers and encouraging words—"Don't settle on the lesser when you can achieve the greater." I love you.

Brianna Nikole "Breeze" Jefferson: I thank you so much for insisting on participating in this project. My goodness, I'm trying to come up with words to acknowledge you.... Beautiful! You are simply beautiful. You understood the importance of this book, and you were careful to capture what you felt. You enthusiastically asked questions and worked hard to share your feelings in your "Special Note." No words can describe my appreciation for your contribution to this book. I thank you so much for believing in me. I was moved by your words because I know they came from your heart. And to think I was supposed to be the teacher/mentor/godfather in this relationship, but I have learned much more from you than you will ever know. You are a beautiful person with a gentle spirit, which makes you strong. Your courage makes you a force to be reckoned with. Do not allow anyone or anything to persuade you, to influence you, or to convince you into thinking otherwise (Little girl, little girl). You were created for a purpose—**PURSUE IT**. Thank you so much for allowing me to be a part of your life. I love you much, gentle Breeze.

Thank you so much, La Quanda and Phillip Barber, for allowing your beautiful daughter, Brianna N. Jefferson, to express herself in this book. You have done an awesome job in guiding her and I am so proud of her. Thank you for allowing me to witness her growth, to share in some of the good times, and lend a helping hand whenever I could. She will make us all very proud. Love you, much!

Last and certainly not the least, to my "Bestie," Minnettia G. Durant: They say true friendship isn't restricted to those we speak to daily. I find this to be true in you. Our friendship is a couple of decades strong, and you have been a strong presence through it all. Thank you for your input, your inspiration, and push with this book. I know without a doubt you are proud of its outcome as I am. I love you much.

A very special thank you to Overseer Jermaine McInnis, Sr. and Senior Executive Pastor Kawana McInnis (Restoration Center of Hope, Brooklyn, New York) for everything you have done to help this project to "get moving." Pastor Kawana: You not only inspired me to go but you led me to the tool needed to move forward.

Dr. Kasim Ali Sidney Jones

Overseer Jermaine: Your hands-on knowledge has been invaluable. May God continue to bless your ministry.

Table of Contents

A Special Note

What can I say about the Reverend Doctor Kasim Ali Sidney Jones? He's my Youth Pastor, my godfather, my friend, and a trustworthy person. I can ask him anything and he will give me an answer. If I don't understand something, he's the man I go to—except for math, but he can count his money. He is a wonderful, outstanding, kindhearted, handsome, tall, sweet person. When I talk to him, he looks me in my face and says what's on his heart. When he's down he never shows it because he hides it behind his smile. Even when I ask what's wrong, he smiles and says, "Nothing Breeze. I'm fine." I don't leave him alone because I know he wouldn't do that to me. I just pray for him like he prays for me.

Reverend Doctor Kasim Ali Sidney Jones is very outstanding. He's a great role model for today's youth. He's very good with teenagers. Dr. Jones is a great role model for me because he saw the path I was on, and cared enough to stop me ahead of time before I made many mistakes I would have regretted. Dr. Jones cared enough to tell me, "I love you too much to let you treat yourself that way." He truthfully told me it was a bad path to go down, and "there are some lessons you don't have to learn the hard way." Dr. Jones, also known as "KJ," is a friend to me. He's a big brother I wish I had, a friend I can tell everything to.

When I asked Dr. Jones for help when I really needed it, I just knew he was going to say yes quickly but he didn't. He sat there quietly and didn't say a word at first. I found out later that he prayed before he said, "Okay, but don't waste your time. You have to learn to help yourself." At first, I didn't want to focus on myself because I didn't take what he was trying to do seriously, but something happened—I saw his heart. He really wanted to help me. One day he told me he was going to stop helping me and I couldn't understand why. He told me, as truthful as he is lots of times: "We're gonna to stop this until you're ready. You can waste your own time, but you're not going to waste my time!" I tried to play it off like I didn't care but he saw that I really did. And then, he sat me down and told me parts of his story when he really didn't have to. When he finished, I convinced him to keep on helping me and he agreed again. I went home and thought about what he said for a while. I decided I could trust him because he really was trying to help me, and I figured it was time for me to help myself. I said to myself, "I can trust him because we both been through some of the same stuff and he understands."

Another thing I can say about the Reverend Doctor Kasim Ali Sidney Jones is that he refuses to give up on me, even when he should. One time he told me, "I know what you're doing and you have to decide if you want to keep on being the victim or not." To be honest, Dr. Jones' honesty hurt sometimes, and I had to learn this the hard way. Sometimes he'll sit back and say nothing, and then, all of a sudden he's right there in my face telling me things I really don't want to hear. I used to cry when he did this because I thought he was a bully. But after being around him for a while I found out he's really not. He is a kindhearted, gentle person. Dr. Jones really cares about me. As a matter of fact, Reverend Doctor Kasim Ali Sidney Jones really loves me, and I love him too.

Reverend Doctor Kasim Ali Sidney Jones shows his

love a lot, and not just for me and my family, but for many other families. A lot of people really don't understand Dr. Jones, but once I saw his heart I knew he really care about children, youth and people, period. He showed my family and me he cares by being there with us, helping us anyway he can, and not complain about it. One morning, my mom called him and told him I was sick. He called back a few minutes later to see if he was dreaming—he's not "a morning person." When my mother told him I was really was sick, he threw on some clothes and rushed to the hospital to see about me. Dr. Jones didn't do this just one time; he did this a few times. I will say to my peers: If you call him, Dr. Jones will really try to help you.

In closing, I am so proud of Reverend Doctor Kasim Ali Sidney Jones—my Youth Pastor, my godfather, my friend, and my big brother. He showed me how to take some things seriously by watching him work on this book and by listening to him talk about it. Dr. Jones really helped me and he really wants to help others. I am so proud to be a part of this book, and I hope it helps you like he helped me. KJ is a person that gives wisdom to the youth. He cares so much about the youth. He does want the best for today's youth. In today's society, our youth is going down the WRONG PATH. If it wasn't for KJ, I think I would be in the same place like other youths. I'm glad he caught me before I got out of hand. I am thankful for him being in my life.

Brianna Nikole "Breeze" Jefferson

March 5, 2014 Atlanta, Georgia

FORWARD

"What counts in life is not the mere fact that we have lived. It is what difference we have made to the lives of others that will determine the significance of the life we lead."

~Nelson Mandela~

Matthew 6:1 says "Take care! Don't do your good deeds publicly, to be admired, because then you will lose the reward from your Father in heaven." ~ The Bible, NLT

I first met Dr. Kasim Jones when we worked under the same counseling organization and both were providing counseling services to clients and families in the home. Our meeting was one that seemed long overdue and once we met a friendship sprouted up so quickly that you would have thought we had known each other for longer than we actually had. Dr. Kasim and I have known one another for about 4.5 years. He is an amazing person, that I am all to happy to call friend, confidant, counselor, Doctor, Mentor and any other name that will help to truly reflect the wonderful, talented, educated, smart, charismatic and beautiful individual that he is.

When we talk about extraordinary people often times we look to those persons that have a certain heir of attention that surrounds them. The ones whose good deeds are often public, the ones who themselves relish in the attention given to them based on the good deeds they have done. Seldom do we automatically look to the people who are quiet and do great deeds day in and day out, as a part of their daily routine, job or nature. These people are the clinicians, social workers, case workers, counselors, and countless others, in addition to regular people who believe in protecting our children and helping families through advocacy, mentoring, linking community resources and more.

Dr. Kasim has a phenomenal gift for working with children and families in need, crisis, and facing trauma from every angle imaginable. That gift has been transformed into amazing works of literature that provide a framework for taking what he has experienced and witnessed in his many years of professional and educational expertise and provides a resource tool to families and individuals seeking answers. This tool can be utilized to teach people how to navigate specific issues that are impacting their lives or the lives of others that they know and care about.

In his first book "No shame in the Game", Dr. Kasim introduces you to the feeling of Shame. From there you get a beautifully, yet simplistic understanding of shame in all its forms. What it looks like, what it sounds like, what it feels like. In reading his first novel I often times found myself so intertwined within the book, that I was remembering relatable scenarios of shame throughout my lifetime, however minor or major they were easily identifiable after reading "No Shame in the Game." Book one was the introduction. In this book Dr. Kasim hits the reader with the unfiltered, truth of shame. Using biblical references and real life cases he has worked, Dr. Kasim breaks down what shame is, what is looks like and the effects of shame on the spirit and the psyche. As the reader pours through the pages they will enter into a darker world of shame associated with sexual assault, something no one likes to talk about. But they will also find solace as you learn how to begin the healing process, steps to take and the journey that will lead to the most powerful healing of all through God.

Inspirational to anyone who reads it, this book shines as a star in a dark sky on how you can overcome the chains of sexual abuse and while relying on God and his love to help restore you to a place of wholeness. You will take a journey that will lead to a vast understanding and a powerful spiritual relationship that brings with it, its own healing. For the professional wanting to tackle a sensitive subject with his clients, to the survivor who is looking for answers, *Tamar's Healing* is a must and a wonderful addition to anyone's library.
~ G.S.WHITE

Preface

Examining the lessons buried within some of those nerve-racking, painful times in your life can be of great use when it comes to moving forward in your life. So many people get "stuck in a rut" in terms of where they are both developmentally and emotionally. I firmly take the position that a person, whether they come to the realization that they are or have been in a toxic, abusive relationship or not, must move pass (mentally and emotionally process) the behaviors that developed during troublesome times in their lives in order to move past their pain and not be stuck. Here is a useful thought:

Each person has a pattern of dealing with grief around loss that is unique to him or her. It grows out of a combination of factors such as modeling early-life losses and experiences around moments of significant life transition... A second factor is how early-life losses and problems were experienced and processed and what meaning we made out of them. If traumatized feelings were worked through and resolved, *we tend to learn from them; if they were not, the unresolved feelings remain within the unconscious, waiting to be triggered by current life issues.* **Hence intense, confusing emotions and distorted meanings become part of our reactive coping pattern in dealing with later loss...** (Dayton, 1997, p. 62, emphasis mine).

I am not suggesting that those whom had been

abused and/or traumatized should jump right into dealing with their issues without help. Receiving guidance and nourishment from someone whom is caring, loving, compassionate, capable, and qualified is highly recommended. However, the first step should start with you and God. I know this was the most important part of my process of forgiving others, and to a certain extent, loving myself again. I had to come to a place where I wanted to stop being angry, because those who hurt me most likely moved on with their lives.

Initially, I blamed others and tried to rationalize why some events happened "to me." For quite some time, I chose not to be involved in intimate relationships because, I did not trust people in general. Eventually, I created walls to protect myself from further harm and damage. I came to find that my isolation created a wider and deeper gap between myself and others. No one was allowed in and I closely monitored what came out. This was my way of circumventing intimacy. I used avoidance whenever someone touched on issues that I refused to explore for myself. As a result, I did not engage in romantic relationships for quite some time. Some people thought my hiatus was a waste of time in that "it was not God-ordained" and I could have simply "gotten over it." By many accounts, these estimations might have had some merit but they did not have the ultimate say. God has the final say on the when and the why I should do this or that. However, I had to choose to allow the healing process to begin within my being.

There was a significant incident that pushed me into what I now call "a deprivation of intimacy," which took place in an environment that was *supposed* to have been a safe place for me when I was about twenty-two. Yet God had a plan for me and a hand on my life. The winters in New Jersey can be treacherously cold and if your windows were old or in bad condition, then your house would be cold. One of the best ways to cut off the draft of a poorly insolated window is to seal it with plastic and tape. This is common amongst people living in this area. One night my brother, my sister-in-law, her older sister, and I went to some friends' house for a holiday party. I was still drinking heavily at that time, and was feeling good by the time the party finally kicked into gear. Some people arrived later that night toting cess (smoking marijuana) in another room in the apartment we were in. Based on my previous run-ins with marijuana, both smoking it and receiving a contact (inhaling it), I needed to get as far away from it as I possibly could. But I did not leave, and could not leave because my brother was my ride home. I chose to stay at the party anyhow. Being that the windows were sealed, it was almost impossible to avoid smelling the marijuana and feeling its wicked effects. After drinking and smelling marijuana for a number of hours, I was extremely inebriated.

The events that transpired later that night ushered in years of pain, anger, resentment, confusion, and most of all, shame. You would have thought the level of danger would have been greater in the apartment where I had been partying, but, it was not. It was in my own home. My plans when I returned home were to take a shower, grab something to eat, and then, go to bed. When I did return home someone was in the bathroom before me, so I sat in the living room, and waited to get into the shower. A "friend" of our family, who was staying with us for a while, approached me with a sexual proposition. Although I was extremely intoxicated, my senses were clear: She was not someone I was interested in sexually. She was like a big sister to me. I managed to avoid her advances for a while, and then I took my shower and got in my bed.

What took place after I went to bed, and the effects of the alcohol and the marijuana once they settled in the worst possible way, remained a mystery for a long time—or was it denial? I woke up the next morning and found my underwear around my left ankle. My first thought was, "I must have fallen asleep while trying to get dressed for bed." But that didn't make sense! I always fully dressed in the bathroom after showering because I lived with women and small children. As I slipped my underwear back on, I noticed moist bodily secretions in my pubic area, which was a clear indication that sexual intercourse had taken place during the night, whether I consented or not.

Filled with denial and shame, I tried not to think about what happened. I did not know what to say or do. I just wanted those thoughts to go away. But I could not avoid the obvious: this "friend" took advantage of me while I was rendered incapable of consenting or declining her advances. I started having flashbacks of what took place that night, which led me to start thinking, "A woman can't rape a man," and "If I told somebody, they'll think I'm a punk or a wimp!" I chose not to use my energy focusing on what happened. Yet there were signs of guilt in the way that this "friend" behaved in my presence. This "friend" appeared to be uncomfortable around me during the last few days she stayed with us. She avoided eye contact with me and made excuses as to why she had to leave the room. I thought it was strange but did not try to overanalyze it.

Within the following week or so, the Holy Spirit started revealing some things I really did not want to accept. On many levels of my self, I knew something did happen that night; and I knew I had to do something to help myself. Nevertheless, I did not do or say anything for a long, long time. I went on a long, perseverating trip of accepting, and then, rejecting the facts, and then, blaming myself for allowing it to happen because "I was a *man* and women can't rape *men*." For a number of years, I refused to admit I needed help processing what happened to me. During this time, I became a "quasi-expert" in making excuses as to why I did not want to be involved in intimate relationships that would have granted others access into my personal space. The real reason was because I was angry, confused, and ashamed.

My healing began once I relocated to Atlanta, Georgia to attend seminary in August 1999. I sought the help of a very capable therapist, Dr. Amy Hartsfield. Remarkably, I started seeing myself differently. I came to the realization that I was not the one driven by lust to force myself upon another person; it was someone else who was so depraved and perverted to carry out such an intrusive act on me. I came across a passage that said, "*If you look for perfect conditions, you will never get anything done. God's ways are as hard to discern as the pathways of the wind, and as mysterious as a tiny baby being formed in a mother's womb*" (Ecclesiastes 11: 4 – 5, NLT). I also began to accept the new life I had received in Christ—"*What this means is that those who become Christians become new persons. They are not the same anymore, for the old life is gone. A new life has begun!*" (2 Corinthians 5: 17, NLT).

Dr. Kasim Ali Sidney Jones

Taken from an earlier work,

Until the Breaking of the Day,

September 6, 2003

K. A. S. J.

Introduction

I had the opportunity to have a real "heart-to-heart" talk with one of my mentees, who I will call "little grasshopper." Little grasshopper was listlessly living without focus or direction, and felt that the timing for this talk was too soon for their taste. Little grasshopper rebuffed and said, "I'm too young for all of that old man stuff," and "I still have a couple of years to go" before they would use the wisdom being imparted. "Hmm," I thought. Needless to say, the timing could not have been more appropriate because I sensed little grasshopper was heading for big time trouble. It was time for me to point out some areas to which little grasshopper demonstrated a lack of direction. Little grasshopper invited me to "tell me about it, ole man," in a sarcastic manner. I let little grasshopper know "I am not as *old* as you think. But if I am *old* to you, I got this *old* for a reason." Little grasshopper was stunned by my remark and sat quietly, listening attentively.

Little grasshopper and I had a lot in common, which was why our mentor/mentee relationship was *interesting* at best. You see, little grasshopper was a sensitive, loving soul, who, sometimes, had a tendency to march to what they believed other people thought or felt about them; therefore, little grasshopper would let things go or not take what was said around or done to them as a means to define who they really were. Little grasshopper also had a tendency to show *a lot* of deception, which set my mind on edge because this could be dangerous in certain situations. But now, little grasshopper was at a place where they were exposing their true self. I knew I had to strike while the coals were hot.

I let little grasshopper know I was not pleased with what I had seen in the past weeks, and did not give little grasshopper time to brace for the impact because they had a tendency to blow me off at times. The phrase little grasshopper repeatedly used when it came time for me to be open and honest with them was: "Oh boy, here you go." I explained that the truth is not designed to say what we wanted to hear, but to let us know what it was, even if it stung. I reminded little grasshopper I was speaking out of love, and not malice. Once I sternly told little grasshopper what was causing me so much heartburn (the pruning), I pointed out some of their positive qualities (the watering/feeding), and then, imported wisdom (fertilizer). I found myself "choking up" and was not surprised by little grasshopper's reactions as we went through this process because they're really sensitive and loving, but did not want everyone to know it. However, I was surprised by how I displayed some of the signs of shame as I had shown before —the shedding of tears, my head hung low, and frequent moments of silence. In the end, I was glad I was able to come into contact with those feelings and share them with little grasshopper; and I am quite sure little grasshopper felt the same because they sat silently and displayed some of the same signs of shame as well.

* * * * *

The overall goal of *Tamar's Healing* is to help bring people out of the darkness of misery and hopelessness into the light of God's glorious love. Far too many people have experienced dark, traumatic events in their lives, and cannot find or see their way out. For many, it grows and festers, and has adverse affects on their lives. Unfortunately, this still rings true today in the African American (Black) community at-large in the United States of America. Even though the behaviors and the circumstances may have changed or might not appear to be germane to the not so distant past in the Black/African American experience in America, the shame has the same lineage. I tried to make this book a "universal," "a non-racial" effort, but I repeatedly returned to address the needs of Black/African Americans. Each time I read statistical findings regarding abuse and the reportings thereof, I felt that these numbers were not truly reflective of those in the African American community. Yet many researchers and authors would agree with a couple of statements: 1.) Shame is a human phenomenon and 2.) Although some of the facial expressions and the emotions felt may appear to be the same, shame is dealt with and articulated differently from culture to culture (Allen, 2010; Bradshaw, 2005; Diederich, 2012; 1993; and Tracy, 2005).

In this book, I will not only address negative, toxic shame, but also speak to healthy, true shame, which is necessary as we journey toward our true selves. That's God's desire for this, God's people. My position is that African (Black) Americans' dealings with shame is a uniquely different phenomena because of the historical "training" or socialization African Americans have acquired and became accustomed to during and since slavery. I truly, staunchly, and adamantly believe most of the statistical information available regarding reported cases of rape, sexual assault, and sexual abuse do not speak for those of African American descent because reporting such incidents may be seen as "airing dirty laundry." This basically means Black folk do not like talking about their problems in the presence of "mixed company"—that is, those who are not their immediate family members, close friends, other relatives or inner circles. But this stronghold must be broken.

Prayerfully, *Tamar's Healing* will help me to "flesh out," so to speak, the concepts and direction I feel God will have me to utilize in order to serve others in the counseling context. Now I will say this up-front: This book is not for the weak hearted, wishy-washy type that repeatedly says they want to move on with their lives, but continue to do, think, and say the same things without trying to initiate or achieve change within their lives. You know the type: "I'm sick and tired of being sick and tired," yet he or she cannot see, hear, feel, or believe there is another way to live! This person will go on choosing the wrong romantic partners, driving cars that are well beyond their means, and even attend a church where they are not being spiritually fed! Someone described this phenomenon as "Living a champagne life on a beer budget." Real change comes from determined individuals who seriously want to do something different. *Tamar's Healing* is for those who want to break some shackles in their lives, and change some things! Change is not for spiritual WHIMPS (yes, I said it). You know the trendy people who pursue the latest cliché or trend, hoping and wishing to find something that is really not for them in the first place. *Tamar's Healing* seeks to dig into some foul places, and pull out dirty, grimy stink that you really want to cover up and hide from the world. You cannot be scared ("SKIRD")! It's for the game changers in the kingdom of God. That is you!

Tamar's Healing will address many types of abuse, but will predominately deal with sexual abuse as depicted in 1 Samuel 13: 1 – 22. Sexual abuse must be discussed more openly because it is still a forbidden subject matter in many African American families and communities. One way we can see this is by the egregious amount of denial that is displayed if or when a Black person tries to reveal sexual abuse in various settings within the Black community, namely their own family. Another way we can see how sexual abuse is a prohibited subject in the Black community is by the way that the person, themselves, behave. Many Black people do not tell others about what happened to them, and this behavior is linked back to slavery. DeGruy (2005) asserted the following words in her book, *Post Traumatic Slave Syndrome*:

> The slave experience was one of continual, violent attacks on the slave's body, mind and spirit. Slave men, women and children were traumatized throughout their lives and the violent attacks during slavery persisted long after emancipation. In the face of these injuries, those traumatized adapted their attitudes and behaviors to simply survive, and these adaptations continue to manifest today (p. 14).

The most alarming aspect of this taboo (sexual abuse) in the Black community is that so many people say they do not have anything to be ashamed of; but oh, my brothers and my sisters, you may not but somewhere amongst your family, your friends, or your associates, it is lurking...! This is because shame keeps it concealed! *Tamar's Healing* will speak to unhealthy shame because there are so many tortured souls haunted by their past and their struggle to cope from one moment to the next. Yet what makes this especially sad is many Christians endure this crippling emotion even more.

As you will see, there are two types of shame—healthy and unhealthy. Healthy shame serves as a regulator, so to speak; while unhealthy, toxic shame acts as a hinderer, a blocker, and a robber of our godly potential. Therefore, I implore you to enter into this place—reading this book—with an open heart and mind, allowing something to reach places you were not certain existed or wish to forget. If you do have something in need of addressing, working out, and walking out; may the Lord God bless and be with you as you travel on your journey toward wholeness.

Tamar's Story

1 Samuel 13: 1 – 22 (New *Living Translation*):

Now David's son Absalom had a beautiful sister named Tamar. And Amnon, her half brother, fell desperately in love with her. [2] Amnon became so obsessed with Tamar that he became ill. She was a virgin, and Amnon thought he could never have her.

[3] But Amnon had a very crafty friend—his cousin Jonadab. He was the son of David's brother Shimea. [4] One day Jonadab said to Amnon, "What's the trouble? Why should the son of a king look so dejected morning after morning?"

So Amnon told him, "I am in love with Tamar, my brother Absalom's sister."

[5] "Well," Jonadab said, "I'll tell you what to do. Go back to bed and pretend you are ill. When your father comes to see you, ask him to let Tamar come and prepare some food for you. Tell him you'll feel better if she prepares it as you watch and feeds you with her own hands."

[6] So Amnon lay down and pretended to be sick. And when the king came to see him, Amnon asked him, "Please let my sister Tamar come and cook my favorite dish as I watch. Then I can eat it from her own hands." [7] So David agreed and sent Tamar to Amnon's house to prepare some food for him.

[8] When Tamar arrived at Amnon's house, she went to the place where he was lying down so he could watch her mix some dough. Then she baked his favorite dish for him. [9] But

when she set the serving tray before him, he refused to eat. "Everyone get out of here," Amnon told his servants. So they all left.

[10] Then he said to Tamar, "Now bring the food into my bedroom and feed it to me here." So Tamar took his favorite dish to him. [11] But as she was feeding him, he grabbed her and demanded, "Come to bed with me, my darling sister."

[12] "No, my brother!" she cried. "Don't be foolish! Don't do this to me! Such wicked things aren't done in Israel. [13] Where could I go in my shame? And you would be called one of the greatest fools in Israel. Please, just speak to the king about it, and he will let you marry me."

[14] But Amnon wouldn't listen to her, and since he was stronger than she was, he raped her. [15] Then suddenly Amnon's love turned to hate, and he hated her even more than he had loved her. "Get out of here!" he snarled at her.

[16] "No, no!" Tamar cried. "Sending me away now is worse than what you've already done to me."

But Amnon wouldn't listen to her. [17] He shouted for his servant and demanded, "Throw this woman out, and lock the door behind her!"

[18] So the servant put her out and locked the door behind her. She was wearing a long, beautiful robe, as was the custom in those days for the king's virgin daughters. [19] But now Tamar tore her robe and put ashes on her head. And then, with her face in her hands, she went away crying.

[20] Her brother Absalom saw her and asked, "Is it true that Amnon has been with you? Well, my sister, keep quiet for now, since he's your brother. Don't you worry about it." So

Tamar lived as a desolate woman in her brother Absalom's house.

[21] When King David heard what had happened, he was very angry. [22] And though Absalom never spoke to Amnon about this, he hated Amnon deeply because of what he had done to his sister.

Part One:

Call It Robbery

Chapter One:

In the Name of Shame

Shame is *not* all bad, negative, destructive, and/or dangerous. Many of us have been trained, socialized and exposed to the harmful side and meaning of shame. To a great extent, shame had been used as a weapon of manipulation by those we believe had our best interests at heart, and this caused more damage than was intended. But the great news is shame is *not* always bad. Too many times our indoctrination is one-sided and guilt-ridden wherein shame is used as a social control apparatus. In other words, a large number of the lessons we learn in our lifetime are aimed at controlling our behavior, and even our way of thinking, in order to conform us to "the norm"—whatever that is. This statement may seem brazen; and it is because it goes against the grain of what is considered the norm. These controls can get in the way of our God-given ability to choose—free will. These controls also open the door to and fortify negative, caustic shame. One decisive step towards promoting free will and abolishing negative shame is to access to information in order to become connected to the will of God. So let's look at shame.

This discussion of shame will be divided into two categories: healthy shame and unhealthy shame. We will begin with healthy shame because it is under-appreciated, and it deserves more attention in our quest toward health and balance. Unhealthy shame should not be addressed without first embracing healthy shame in the process.

It Is What It Is: Healthy/True Shame

The first step toward health and balance is to acknowledge and accept that some shame is good for us. In fact, Smedes (1993) noted: "Shame is not necessarily a bad thing to feel. Shame can get us in touch with the most beautiful part of our self. It can also be a warning that we are becoming the kind of person we do not really want to be." Now that is great news! We feel this warning whenever we encounter a situation where we have done something that is truly not in our true character. When this is encountered, we feel bad and either apologize or repent (ask for forgiveness from God and turn away from it), and carefully move on with our lives, trying not to repeat that behavior again. At least that should be the goal.

Healthy shame provides balance and the ability to flourish, even within our limits. Bradshaw (2005) explained this ability in the following:

Healthy shame lets us know that we are limited. It tells us that to be human is to be limited. Actually, humans are *essentially* limited. *Not one of us has, or can ever have, unlimited power...* Limitation is our essential nature. Grave problems result from refusing to accept our limits... Healthy shame is an emotion that teaches us about our limits. Like all emotions, shame moves us to get our basic needs met... Healthy shame is part of every human's personal power. It allows us to know our limits, and thus to use our energy more effectively. We have better direction

3

when we know our limits. We do not waste ourselves on goals we cannot reach or on things we cannot change. Healthy shame allows our energy to be integrated rather than diffused (p. 7, 8).

Being limited by our humanness carries with it the need for certain acknowledgements, especially as Christians: God is the source of our being. Everything we do by faith in Jesus the Christ comes into fruition, and we have an eternal guide—the Holy Spirit—to lead us along the way—"For in him we live and move and have our being...." (Act 17:28, *NIV*). Again, that's great news!

How did such a concept of healthy shame come into being? "God, in his mercy, created human beings," Allen (2010) noted, "with a capacity to feel the remorse of shame whenever we engage in behaviors and attitudes that are hurtful to others or ourselves. This *good* shame is a blessing that it encourages surrender to God's healing grace and power" (p. x). It is my belief that all of us have a general understanding of what is right and what is wrong; however, we do not interpret or value these concepts in the same fashion. Therefore, we all feel remorse differently, if at all, in various situations. That is the free will that was given to us all. Malone (2006), in his explanation of "true shame," discussed healthy shame this way:

> True shame is what we experience when we sin and are aware of it—that awful feeling of having missed the mark or failed, regret that we have disappointed God and/or other people. In those circumstances,

God has allowed shame to come to draw us back to Him. Like Adam in the Garden of Eden, we have two options. We can run and hide or we can acknowledge our sin, repent of it, and ask God to forgive us. Our fellowship is restored" (p. 3).

I strongly agree with Malone because healthy shame is designed to provide a sort of "checks-and-balances" system to our consciousness and our lives. Yet Malone (2006) continued on to say, "Our Creator has many emotions, and He created us to experience and give expression to them— sadness, joy, anxiety, psychological pain, or even physical expressions like tapping your foot, clapping your hands or snapping your fingers" (p. 5). Therefore, if God has created us with the same feelings that God has, then, what does this say about our entire being? Tracy (2005) answered this question in a concise manner:

The point is that healthy shame is based on our unique dignity as bearers of God's image. No matter how we've sinned, healthy shame is a gracious call to correction and cleansing so we can be what the Lord of the universe meant us to be. In other words, healthy shame sounds an internal foghorn that we are headed toward to jagged rocks. It is a gracious call to repentance. It's the basis for calling believers to lovingly practice church discipline on fellow believers who are engaged in ongoing sinful behavior, so that they will be shamed and prompted to repent (p. 75).

Healthy shame is a great asset to possess because to have no shame equates to having no sense of right and wrong. Allen (2010) explained it this way: "...to be shameless is to have no conscience or a faulty moral development. This leads to corruption and fragmentation" (p. 21). In other words, healthy shame signifies something is wrong or that we are not acting in such a way that is pleasing to God, or that we are behaving contrary to whom we were created to be. Bradshaw (1995) used the concept of "shamelessness" as he discussed toxic shame and offered two explanations when he wrote:

> Shamelessness takes two forms: We act shameless by attempting to transcend our limits as human beings; we try to be more than human—we act perfect (we never make mistakes), we act needless (we need n help from anyone), we act righteous (we are saved and others are not), we act authoritarian (we have the right to violate others' space), we act patronizing (we know it all).... At the other extreme we can act shameless by acting less than human. We let others violate us or we violate ourselves. We become shameful failures, victims, addicts—the dregs of society. We are so hopeless, we lose all sense of limits. We believe that everything about us is flawed and defective (p. 29).

God created us to be more than just our actions. Healthy shame brings us to a place that helps us to reflect on who and whose we are. Smedes (1993) wrote, "It is good to know that we have a better self to be called back to, and it is good to know that our shame is perhaps the surest sign of our divine origin and our human dignity. When we feel this sense of shame, we are feeling a nudge from our *true selves*" (p. 32; emphasis mine). I would like to think that we all have some divine elements within our beings, and we can to tap into them when needed. However, it is difficult to explain why some choose to do things that are evil in the sight of God.[1] Smedes (1993) continued on to elucidate on the concept of the "true self" when he wrote:

> Our true self is like the design for a building still under construction or the original design for a building that needs restoring. It is stamped in the depths of us like a template for the selves we are meant to be and yet are failing to be... Our actual self—the self we are from day to day—never quite matches the template of our true self. In fact, the gap between our true self and our actual self is what creates our healthy feelings of shame (p. 32).

Taking these things into consideration, healthy shame also creates room for us to enhance our character and moral development. Allen (2010), in his landmark work, *Shame: The Human Nemesis*, wrote, "Constructive shame implies having a conscience so that when we do wrong, we feel shame, seek to correct it, make amends, and then the shame is removed" (p. 21). In his treatment of shame, Kaufman (1996) also succinctly spoke of healthy shame in the following, powerful fashion: "Shame alerts us not only to transgression but also to any affront to human dignity. By motivating the eventual correction of social indignities, shame plays a vital positive role" (p. 5). Once this positive shame warns us that we are

---

[1] For a biblical perspective, see Romans 1.

out of line, we become aware that we should get things in order. It does not matter if the "indignity" is of significance or is lower on the pecking order; healthy shame signals the need for an adjustment in our behavior, our attitude and/or our treatment of others.

From a Christian point of view, healthy shame not only provides us with an internal regulating system where it brings about feelings of regret and guilt due to our actions and/or thoughts, it signals our need for restoration and reconciliation to God, which can be achieved through repentance, and reconnecting to our true selves. Tracy (2005) boldly yet clearly illustrated this reality from a biblical perspective:

> The basic biblical concept of shame is emotional humiliation due to sin, which results in human or divine disgrace and rejection. Shame in Scripture carries similar connotations to its modern usage—a painful emotional sense of guilt, unworthiness, and disgrace due to one's failure to live up to a standard... but unlike secular psychological descriptions of shame that define it purely in terms of subjective human experience, biblical shame is ultimately defined by the character of God... Thus, the key to overcoming shame is more than simply learning to love and accept oneself; it is to discern God's perspective on one's shame and guilt, and to let his perspective drive and reshape one's thoughts, action, and, ultimately, one's feelings... Biblically, shame is not just an emotional or psychological reality but a judicial one as well, for human emotional experience is not always concordant

8

with one's spiritual condition (p. 83).

The Set Up: Unhealthy/False/Toxic Shame

There is an important point to be made about guilt and shame as I transition onto to my discussion of unhealthy shame. For most people, guilt and shame are one in the same, but they are not. Tracy (2005) asserted, "The critical difference between healthy and unhealthy (toxic) shame is the relationship between shame and guilt" (p. 75). Guilt is a person doing something wrong and knowing it. In fact, "Guilt is a moral/legal state that results from having violated the law, thus rendering one liable to a penalty" (p. 75). Therefore, guilt is a logical, cognitive process that is the result of our actions; while shame is the feeling resulting from those actions. Tracy surmised:

> Shame is the painful emotional response to the perception of being guilty. Thus, healthy shame is an appropriate response to an actual violation of the law of God. It is a divine gift because it signals that something is dreadfully wrong, that we are not living up to our created design, and that we are alienated from our loving, holy Creator (Tracy, 2005, p. 75).

Unhealthy or toxic shame has been described in a number of ways. Allen (2010) called it the *"Master Emotion"* because, "It combines the powerful affects of anger, hurt, remorse, rejection, abandonment, and humiliation" (p. 17). In fact, Malone (2006) discussed the concept of the "Master

Emotion" in the ensuing way: "Shame has been a 'master emotion' because it binds itself to other emotions, especially when they are denied or repressed" (p. 4). Shame, unhealthy and toxic shame, can prompt a myriad of triumphs as well as disappointments. Therefore, we must be able to discern what is occurring within ourselves. Allen (2010) further said this regarding the Master Emotion: "Shame can spur major achievements or create unthinkable and devastating violence" (p. 27).

Through the years, unhealthy toxic shame has garnered a long list of images. Smedes (1993) said "shame is a very heavy feeling" (p. 5). So simple yet so true because you have to carry injurious shame around like a ton of bricks. In my experience with toxic shame, when it comes on strong, it is quite difficult to maneuver around it. This arduous maneuvering leads to what Smedes described as inadequacies, in short,

It is [shame is] a feeling that we do not measure up and maybe never will measure up to the sorts of persons we are meant to be. The feeling, when we are conscious of it, gives us a vague disgust with ourselves, which in turn feels like a hunk of lead on our hearts... Almost everybody feels shame sometimes, like an invisible load that weighs our spirits down and crushes out our joy. It is a lingering sorrow. But it can also be an acute pain that stings you at the moment you are feeling best (pp. 5-6).

Yet, in all of this, this heaviness oftentimes leaves one

feeling worthless. It also continues to fester in one's spirit to depths that may appear to be incurable and hopeless. Every mistake, shortcoming, and letdown only adds to a shame-laden person's sense of worthlessness—if that makes sense? Welch (2012) makes this plain when he wrote: "The message is clear: you have fallen short, you don't measure up. Other people are acceptable, you are not. They succeed, you fail. They are good, you are bad. They are important, and you are disposable. It is all about value and worth. The shamed person feels worthless in the eyes of others and worthless before God" (p. 29). This is not true at all!

Toxic shame takes lead over one's emotions—thus becoming the Master Emotion—and diminishes one's faith or willingness to believe that he or she deserves their humanity. "Shame is the deep sense that you are unacceptable," as Welch (2012) explained, "because of something you did, something done to you, or something associated with you. You feel exposed and humiliated" (p. 2). When people engage in self-destructive behaviors, we would oftentimes attribute their behavior to poor self-esteem or low self-worth, or they're just bad people. However, underneath it all there may be a powerful, deep seated presence of toxic shame, whether it is real or imagined by that person. In his discussion about unhealthy shame, Malone (2006) asserted, "false shame (also called toxic shame) is a tool of Satan" (p. 4). Now this is a profound revelation because, like many things of God, the devil tries to extort what is good to meet his own ends. When a person is vulnerable or if they are in a weakened state, he or she can become susceptible to being used by the devil. Malone continued on to write the following statement:

11

It is a fear of being found out, being abandoned or rejected, being exposed or exposing other. False shame is the lie we believe about ourselves, the rejection of God's love and forgiveness based on feelings of personal unworthiness. It will keep us from vulnerability and healing (p. 4).

With this fear of being identified or labeled, depending on the individual, a person may experience severe struggles while trying to amass the strength to rebound and reconnect with their true self. Allender (2008) declared, "Shame has been called by Jean-Paul Sartre a hemorrhage of the soul" (p. 61). This hemorrhage, this severe bleeding, the draining of the soul, can come in the form of destructive behaviors. I recall the axiom that says: "Actions speak louder than words." Surely this applies to the human condition and shame. Welch (2012) expressed the affects of self-destructive behaviors in a shame-based person in the subsequent fashion:

Sometimes with shame there are no words. Shame takes us to the extremes where words fall short, so we express shame by doing disgusting things. Intentional vomiting and degrading promiscuity can be part of it. Less degrading, though just as effective, is intentional failure in work or relationships. Yes, shame can deliberately undermine any possible success. If you catch a whiff of something good, you treat it as a threat. You run from it, drink at it, drug at it, sabotage it.... People who live with shame believe they don't deserve anything good. Sure, others get hurt by shame's self-destructive ways, but it's not as if you wanted to hurt them. You are doing your loved ones a favor (you think) if you distance yourself from

12

them. You will ruin lives eventually, so you might as well get it over with (p. 32).

All of this is to say: unhealthy, toxic, false shame can be detrimental to one's soul, to one's spirit. It is as deadly as gangrene or cancer, for it eats away at one's humanity. I will end this chapter regarding unhealthy toxic shame with the following quote from Bradshaw's (2005) *Healing the Shame that Binds You*:

> The feeling of shame has the same demonic potential to encompass our whole personality. Instead of the momentary feeling of being limited, making a mistake, littleness, or being less attractive or talented than someone else, a person can come to believe that *his[or her] whole self is fundamentally flawed* and defective... Internalized or toxic shame lethally disgraces us to the point where we have no limits or boundaries (pp. 21 – 22).

Chapter Two:

Innocence as a Target

Now David's son Absalom had a beautiful sister named Tamar. And Amnon, her half brother, fell desperately in love with her. [2] Amnon became so obsessed with Tamar that he became ill. She was a virgin, and Amnon thought he could never have her.

[3] But Amnon had a very crafty friend—his cousin Jonadab. He was the son of David's brother Shimea. [4] One day Jonadab said to Amnon, "What's the trouble? Why should the son of a king look so dejected morning after morning?"

So Amnon told him, "I am in love with Tamar, my brother Absalom's sister."

<u>Carry This Weight</u>

From the beginning of Tamar's story, clearly there was a problem. Verse 1a says, "Now David's son Absalom had a beautiful sister named Tamar." This opening line instantly shows an obvious detachment between Tamar and her father, King David, for she was said to be the sister[2] of Absalom, a prince, a son of King David. Tracy (2005) said it this way: "…this story begins by deftly introducing pregnant phrases that will soon turn sinister. The careful reader will quickly feel something is amiss in this family" (p. 56). Straight away, you can see how Tamar was presented as an object of beauty, a thing, an entity, possessed rather than

---

[2] See 2 Samuel 3:3.

owned as the princess that she was; bringing about an element of shame to her. Lewis (1995) described this phenomenon in these terms:

> ...shame-eliciting events is the belief that shame is a state of self-devaluation that can, but does not have to, emanate from "out there." Shame for her involves self-consciousness and self-imagery, that is, the idea of the other's feelings. She distinguishes shame, which is about the self, from guilt, which is about action related to another... While it is true that she suggests that shame arises out of, and in large part is caused by, the loss of approval of a significant other, the source of the shame is out thoughts about our selves. The stimulus eliciting the state is self-thought about the self (p. 32).

In other words, Tamar probably felt lower than she really was, both socially and personally, because of how she was portrayed by others, especially by her father the king, her family members, and the community at-large. Tamar was probably afforded all of the amenities of a princess, but what she really needed was to be cared for. "Care means," as Stone (2004) wrote, "tending to their emotional needs, too. It means honoring them and respecting their rights... It means embracing them and listening to them and letting them know that nothing is more important than what they have to say" (p. 18). This is a powerful foundation for our children, and Tamar may have longed for this kind of care.

During early socialization, messages are learned by the individual helps to establish a foundation for growth and adjustments to many situations that he or she may encounter at different stages of their lives. One would learn who they are and how to identify with others. In fact, Kaufman (1992) explained this phenomenon this way: "Identification begins within the family. Learning how to become a person originates through identification, as we first identify and thereby have a beginning base from which to navigate the human world" (p. 38). For Tamar, she was most likely called beautiful a lot but not treated beautifully. It is very probable that Tamar's siblings witnessed how she was treated and followed suit by treating her the same way. In this sense, this kind of environment created a license to mistreat Tamar because of her family's structure. Some members failed to see that Tamar was more than beautiful "eye candy." She was a person who deserved to be treated with dignity and respect. Instead, those around her did as Kaufman explained: "Interpersonal learning in the family becomes the model for the gradually unfolding relationship which the self comes to have with the self" (p. 99). Therefore, not only did Tamar suffer from her family's attitude and perception of her, the entire family unit participated in and perpetuated the mistreatment of Tamar.

Although the Bible does not clearly indicate Tamar's expression of her needs and/or wants, she most certainly needed to be acknowledged as a person; not just someone's beautiful half-sister. In fact, Tamar had a right to be identified as King David's daughter, a princess! Tracy (2005) declared this lack of acknowledgement in this way: "...Absalom and Amnon are identified as sons of David, but Tamar is simply Absalom's sister. This is odd, since Tamar is the daughter of King David and Queen Maacah (2 Samuel 3:

3). In fact, nowhere in the entire account is Tamar ever referred to as the daughter of David" (p. 56). Enough said!

Imagine, if you will, being the sibling or the child who is always referred to by a physical feature or a connection to someone else, or being linked to your parents. For example, longhaired Sally, knocked-kneed Frank, John-John's cousin, or Billy's boy. Can you relate to how a person might feel when they are constantly referred to through someone else? Are you able to connect with this person's need, desire, yearning to be who they are as an individual? I can relate with how Tamar must have felt because I, too, was distanced from my own father until my late twenties. For many years, I was the youngest of four boys and a preacher's kid. People made a point of associating me with either my mother— "That's Shirley's little boy"—or my brothers—"Oh, he's Willie's, Roy's or Duane's little brother." Sometimes hearing "little" attached to my name made my blood boil. Even then, I knew I needed to be acknowledged in my own right. For a long time I did things on my own terms. I rebelled and did some of the things that went against what I was taught. My antics were not always good or healthy, but my behavior and attitude was my way of bumping the system and growing into my own person. I did many things, the way I did them, because they were my decisions to make. And this growth was agitated by the shame I felt as a result of my own behavior. But Tamar... A lot of her stuff in this story came from others, and she struggled to find her own way.

Yet, in the first few verses, no one really took ownership of Tamar, they possessed her. Reread verses 1 through 4 again. And then, carefully pay attention to the way Tamar was referred to as this story proceeds. One gets the sense that Tamar was a rejected child and person. Smedes (1993) articulated the difference between ownership and possession of a child or person in the following manner:

> If we possess something, we can control it, use it, neglect it, and get rid of it as the mood strikes. This is why only lifeless things may be possessed. But if we own a person, we give her our commitment of an unconditional love and thereby tell her that she will never be disowned, never rejected, never despised… The difference between owning and possessing comes down to this: we possess things, but we own persons. We do whatever we wish with what we possess. We treat a person we own as the Godlike and therefore inviolable being he or she is. Possession is control; ownership is commitment… Feeling owned, I contend, is love's way to immunize a child against shame. Now I want to explain how feeling dis-owned is the seed-bed of shame (pp.69-70, 71).

I was absolutely floored when I first read this passage for the first time. So much so that I had to read it three or four times to be sure of what I read. When it comes to the words "own" and "possess," my mind automatically shifted to other powerful things because of the a cultural context of my upbringing. I grew up in a lower middle-class neighborhood—and many times even lower than that—

where families struggled, worked, and struggled some more just to make it day-by-day. To own or possess things, let alone people, which also incited thoughts of slavery, was not a luxury we were afforded very often, if at all. Yet, as it is applied to people, and not in a subjugated fashion as in slavery, owning and possessing made sense. As Smedes (1993) explained, "Feeling owned, I contend, is love's way to immunize a child against shame" (p. 71). Amen!

Tamar's description in the first four verses of this biblical account gives us hints as to how she may have been reared in the royal palace. She could have received all of the amenities afforded to the royal family members, but it was the emotional attachment and support she needed from significant others. King David was her father and that may have been the bottom line for her. It is likely that she wanted the simplest things from King David—a hug, a smile, or a wink of his eye. As it appears, these wishes went unfulfilled for Tamar. Bradshaw (2005) challenged parents and caregivers of children in this moving fashion:

Part of the work of love is listening. Children are clear about what the need and will tell us in no uncertain terms. We need to listen to them. This requires a fair amount of emotional maturity. To listen well, one must have one's needs met. If one is needy, it's hard to listen. Our neediness is like a toothache. When we are shame-based, we can only focus on our own aches... Needy, shame-based parents cannot possibly take care of their children's needs. The child is shamed whenever he or she is needy because the child's needs clash with the parents' needs. The child grows up and becomes an adult. Bu underneath the mask of adult behavior there is a child who was neglected. Needy children are insatiable. They have a hole in their soul created by unresolved grief and development dependency deficits. This makes them adult children... [Get this!] Needy children need parents, so adult children turn lovers in parents, someone to take care of their needs (pp. 46, 47).

This suggestive prodding is especially needed as it applies to children of African descent. Let us look at Grier and Cobbs' (2000) treatment of achieving womanhood as it relates to Black girls and women:

In the world of women an abundance of feminine narcissism is not only a cheerful attribute but a vital necessity to emotional well-being. For a woman to invite and accept the love of a man whom she respects, she must feel herself to be eminently worthy of his interest and, in a deep and abiding sense, loveable person. Such a conviction carries with it a compelling confidence grown out of the loving engagement of a mother with her precious child, of a family with a delightful little girl, and a larger community likewise charmed by her. With these benevolent auspices, augmented by real physical attractiveness, the stage is set for the growth and development of a self-confident woman who can enter wholeheartedly into love relationships, bringing a richness and a warmth to her mate and to the children who from their union (pp. 39 – 40).

As you can see, there is a correlation between the relationship with the parent and the child, and the needs or neediness of that parent. In the quotation above, it is geared toward the Black mother and their daughter. The "feminine narcissism" deals with the natural female drive to receive attention in a healthy way. Do not let the word narcissism distract you from this point, because it leads to a pertinent point. The phrase "augmented by real physical attractiveness, the stage is set for the growth and development of a self-confident woman…" tells a lot about how the Black girl learns to engage the world around her. Too many Black girls are taught both directly and indirectly, to use their sex appeal to get what she wants and needs. Far too many Black women-children are left to fend for themselves. This grows out of the relationship the Black female child has with her mother and other female caretakers. Grier and Cobbs (2000) further explained this relationship in the following manner:

The first measure of a child's worth is made by her mother, and if, as is the case with so many black people in America, that mother feels that she herself is a creature of little worth, this daughter, however valued and desired, represents her scorned self. Thus the girl can be loved and valued only within a limited sphere, and can never be the flawless child, because she is who she is—black and inevitably linked to her black, depreciated mother—always seen to be lacking, deficient, and faulty in some way. Nor can the family or the community at large undo this attitude, since children, however wonderful they may be to adults, are always seen in terms of the future, and in this country the future of a dark girl is dark indeed.... ....[As bleak and limited as it is] she takes her place within a historical context, in which women like her have never been valued, have been viewed only as depreciated sexual objects who serve as the recipients of certain debased passions of men who are ashamed to act them out with their own women. Historically she has had some value as a "breeder" of slaves and workmen. But most of all she has been viewed, as all black people have been viewed, as a source of labor: and she has been valued for the amount of work she can perform (pp. 40, 41).

Although this is a lengthy quotation, it covers areas that other sources cannot because of their cultural contextual naiveté— either they are not Black, or they were not exposed to a variety of Black families. Let's continue looking at the Black mother/daughter relationship. If the mother's concept of herself is faulty and/or flawed, she will be ill-equipped to assist her daughter in becoming a balanced woman, who can achieve a healthy amount of feminine narcissism. In other words, a mother who does not feel good about herself, for whatever reason, will most likely prove to be ineffective in helping her daughter feel good about herself; especially if that mother is a shame-based person. The daughter, in turn, will most likely rely on her physical attractiveness to send false messages regarding how she feels about herself, which is a depreciated sense and use of her sexuality, rendering her objectified as a sexual thing or instrument. This is what I believe happened to Tamar.

I had a distressing conversation with a person who was concerned about a good friend of theirs and her daughter. This person's friend was described as "a sweet person, who means well," the person said, "but I'm afraid she is not equipped to meet her daughter's needs—intellectually and emotionally." With such a loaded statement as this, I was instantly interested in what this person had to say. This person continued on to say, "You can't expect her (the mother) to help her child when she (the daughter) has already exceeded her mother." To clarify, I asked this person to say more about the daughter exceeding her mother. "Well, intellectually the child has reached a place where her mother is not able to help her because she (the mother) has not achieved it for herself," the other person said with passion. This person went on to express their hope for someone to assist both the mother and her child, "because if she (the mother) is not careful she (the daughter) can make mistakes that will complicate her (the daughter's) future."

How does this relate to Tamar? Returning to Grier and Cobbs' (2000) explanation of "Achieving Womanhood" in their classic book *Black Rage*:

However beautiful she might be in a different setting with different standards, in this country she is ugly. However loved and prized she may be by her mother, family, and community, she has no real basis of feminine narcissism. When to her physical unattractiveness is added a discouraging, depreciating mother-family-community environment into which she is born, there can be no doubt that she will develop a damaged self-concept and an impairment of her feminine narcissism which will have profound consequences for her character development (p. 41).

Do you recall the phrase: Tamar's beauty became a source of pain? This quote certainly sheds some light on Tamar's situation. Tamar's beauty became something that attracted ugly actions and sentiments from others. No matter how much other people around her may have believed she was prized and valued because of her beauty, Tamar had no chance of achieving a healthy level of personhood and womanhood; therefore, Tamar's character was damaged before she had a chance to grow into her true self. Tamar needed more from her family and her community.

Members of a royal family are groomed and trained on how to carry themselves as members of that royal family, even if that family has problems. In situations such as this decorum oftentimes outweigh the needs of the individual. We probably can speculate that Tamar was trained to be a beautiful princess and a dutiful wife. I cannot imagine how this situation could have been for her, but I can accurately say most of Tamar's dutiful grooming came from her mother, Queen Maacah (2 Samuel 3: 3). In many ways, this is useful and it has its place; however, it can also be damaging to the individual, especially when that prince or princess is not the heir apparent or not close in line to the throne.

In the case of royal families, specifically the female members, individuality may not be encouraged or tolerated. If Queen Maacah was brought up in this type of climate, she may not have developed what Grier and Cobbs (2000) called "healthy female narcissism," where she developed her own individuality. This was probably was so in Tamar's relationship with her mother, Queen Maacah. This lends to our understanding of how Tamar was possibly objectified.

Not Like That…

As this biblical account continues, we are able to see the direction Tamar traveled. By her emotional needs not being met by significant others, namely her father, King David, she was vulnerable, open to attack from others. Amnon must have recognized this vulnerability. Verse two illustrates how Amnon begin to express his lascivious desires for a *thing* that was his sister. You see, this story captures different forms of abuse along with the obvious sexual assault of Tamar. This is why we owe it to our children to help them express themselves in healthy ways in order to help them to avoid abusing others and being abuse by others. In other words, we must teach our children, both male and female, restraint! We must teach our children that their urges and other yearnings are as natural to life as breathing, but prioritizing should be taught as well—counting up the cost for instant or quick gratification or delaying what can wait until later. And in today's society, with the strong pull of the music, videos, and/or social media our children listen to and are exposed to that is offered to them, we owe it to our children to instill a solid foundation for them to refer to when they are out of our reach.

In many ways, a double standard prevails in our families and communities. We want to keep our girls "pure," while encouraging our boys to "sow your wild oats." Question: Where will our boys sow their oats if the girls are *supposed* to be pure? Tracy (2005) explained it this way:

> In highly patriarchal families, female children are often given less protection and honor than their male siblings. It's also strange that the story begins by mentioning Absalom first, since Amnon was the royal prince who would succeed David on the throne and thus would normally be honored by being mentioned first... Unfortunately for Tamar, **she ends up a pawn** in a family power play... ...*The needs of individual family members are highly expendable.* The weak members of a family can be used up and exploited to feed the appetites of the more powerful family members (p. 56, bold emphasis mine).

So if this happens to female children in "highly patriarchal families," how does the male children come to receive what is *perceived* as more protection and honor? I place emphasis on perceived because we have to keep in mind that the number of reported instances of sexual abuse and/or confirmed abuse of black males is significantly lower because of the under-reporting phenomena (not telling or not "snitching") in many Black communities. On top of this "no snitch" code in many Black communities, the male ego comes into play when it comes to reporting, talking about, or admitting to being violated. Again, we must consider slavery in this context because, believe it or not, some of its remnants can be found somewhere in the layers of dysfunction, for a

26

lack of better words, plaguing the African American psyche. However, Grier and Cobbs (2000) offered some information that may be useful for our understanding:

> ...the black boy in growing up encounters some strange impediments. Schools discourage his ambitions, training for valued skills is not available to him, and when he does triumph in some youthful competition he receives compromised praise, not the glory he might expect. In time he comes to see that society has locked arms *against* him, that rather than help he can expect opposition to his development, and that he lives not in a benign community but in a society that views his growth with hostility.... As boys approach adulthood, masculinity becomes more and more bound up with money making. In a capitalistic society economic wealth is inextricably interwoven with manhood. Closely allied is power— power to control and direct other men, power to influence the course of one's own and other lives. The more lives one can influence, the greater the power. The ultimate power is the freedom to understand and alter one's life. It is this power, both individually and collectively, which has been denied the black man (pp. 58 – 59, 60).

At first glance, some of the above statements may seem to be dated or irrelevant in this day and age. But stop for a moment and ask yourself, are these statements obsolete and inapplicable in today's society? Do they speak to the present African American condition? If you said yes, look at what the authors (Grier and Cobbs, 2000) wrote about myths and stereotypes regarding Black Americans, when they wrote:

> The mythology and folklore of black people is filled with tales of sexually prodigious [abnormal, phenomenal] men. Most boys grow up on a steady diet of folk heroes who have distinguished themselves by sexual feats... Dreams must in some way reflect reality, and in this country the black man, until quite recently, had not been in positions of power. His wielding of power had been in the privacy of the boudoir... But where sex is employed as armament and used as a conscious and deliberate means defense, it is the black man who chooses this weapon. If he cannot fight the white man openly, he can and does battle him secretly. Recurrently, the pattern evolves of black men using sex as a dagger to be symbolically thrust into the white man (p. 64).

Hmm, the last few lines caused me to scratch my chin in wonderment. But consider this for now, *black men using sex to fight white men....* For me it's a bit of a stretch because I can only see it in one way: Black men are dating and marrying more white women recently. If that counts for using their daggers to "symbolically thrust into the white man" than have at it. This subject will be discussed in greater detail in later chapters.

If It Is, It Ain't

Let us return to Tamar and her story. I left off where Amnon was lusting after Tamar. You should be able to see how Tamar was counted amongst the "lesser valued" people in her family because Amnon saw and plotted against her as if she was a thing to be conquered or acquired. It is shockingly fascinating when you look at the depraved mind when it focuses on people whom are trying to do the right thing or are innocent. They befriend them and gain their trust only to taint and corrode them. You see Amnon was conceited, arrogant, and "entitled" because he was next in line to become king, while Tamar was way down the totem pole in their family. To Amnon, Tamar did not have much value, hieratically. But she was a child of the king just as Amnon was! Are you seeing how this is starting to line up? More attention and protection is provided to those who are valued in the family and society.

The second part of verse two says, "She [Tamar] was a virgin, and Amnon thought he could never have her." This line tells us that Amnon's intentions were not pure because he could have *had* Tamar if his intentions were honorable. In other words, Amnon could have asked for Tamar's hand in marriage, but that was not what he wanted. He wanted sex, a cheap thrill, a sexual release at Tamar's expense. Nevertheless, he lusted after her and allowed his degenerate desires take control of his heart and mind. So Amnon took it to another level, he recruited others to help him to achieve his goal—to abuse, to violate Tamar's body, and to mutilate of her soul. For Tamar, her beauty would become the source of agony. Tracy (2005) eloquently wrote: "Beauty metastasizes into pain and shame. Brotherly love turns out to be bestial lust. What you thought was the safest place on earth—your own family home—turns out to be the most dangerous" (p. 56).

Tamar could not help being born who she was. She never asked to be beautiful nor did she ask to be born into the family she was a part of. "No wonder," Tracy (2005) continued on to say, "those who grow up in abusive families find it nearly impossible to trust their own perceptions and emotions. No wonder so many abuse victims are so confused they feel they are going insane. Most are quite sane, but they live in insane families" (p. 56). What more can be said?

In wisdom, I discovered something that helped me to arrive at a critical place in my comprehension of many things that transpire within some families—including my own family—WHAT IS "NORMAL" FOR ME MAY NOT BE "NORMAL" FOR SOMEONE ELSE. What this means is, simply put, just because my family or household functions in a certain fashion does not give me the right to judge another person's or family's method of doing things and vice versa. However, there is a line that cannot be crossed, legally. In many families, unfortunately, abuse is an everyday occurrence. To take it a little further, too many families live in a perpetual state of denial or simply refuse to deal with the abuse, especially sexual abuse, which is happening right under their noses. Stone (2004) straightforwardly addressed what is "a dereliction of parental duties" when she wrote, "Sexual abuse is a violation of that unspoken family trust.. And when we look the other way or don't call out a situation of abuse, then we too are breaking the family trust" (p. 18).

This is a taboo that continues in Black families today. We would like to think that it does not happen to "our own," and, therefore, it still remains something that should not be talked about. This can be and is considered neglect, especially if the abuse is known and nothing is done about it. According to Georgia Social Services Manual (2008), neglect is defined as "Failure of a parent/caretaker to provide adequate food, clothing, shelter, medical care, supervision or *emotional* care for a child to whom they are responsible…." (p. 9, emphasis mine). In other words, parents and caretakers have a *legal* responsibility to care for their children's needs. In the state of Georgia's law defines neglect in the ensuing manner:

> Neglect or exploitation of a child by a parent or caretaker if said neglect or exploitation consists of a lack of supervision, abandonment, or intentional or unintentional disregard by a parent or caretaker of a child's basic needs for food, shelter, medical care, or education as evidenced by repeated incidents or a single incident which places the child at substantial risk of harm" **(O.C.G.A. § 49-5-180(5)(B).**

31

It is really an unfortunate reality that a large number of parents/caretakers need this type of information to consider their way of doing things in regards of the care (or lack of care) they provide to their own children. Again, this is not to judge anyone, but it is simply a truth that must be presented in our communities. There are times and situations where the parents may not know that their parenting methods may be harmful to the child. One credo comes to mind: He or she needs to toughen up because it's a cold world out there. Faulty parenting methods may be that parent's way of giving their child the security blanket that the parent feels the child will need to survive. However, this security blanket may be cruel and illegal under the eyes of the law in most states.

Returning to the story of Tamar, Amnon lusted after her and constantly thought of ways to "have her," as in procuring her. Verse three says, "But Amnon had a very crafty friend—his cousin Jonadab." By all indications, we can pretty much tell something menacing is about to happen in this story. Amnon itched so badly for Tamar that he began to enlist other people without them knowing his motives, which were self-centered to the highest degree. Here is how Tracy (2005) illustrated this situation:

> Amnon was specifically said to be frustrated because Tamar was a virgin and it was "hard …to do anything to her." This probably refers to the fact that royal virgins were kept under close guard, so Amnon was not able to have sexual relations with her. Amnon's "love" was nothing more than an incestuous lust he had fanned into a fire. The irony here is that Amnon made himself sick with his own lust for his sister,

Amnon, Jonadab, and David (with varying degrees of knowledge) all placed the responsibility on Tamar to heal Amnon's self-induced sickness. *In abusive families, the victim is made responsible for solving needs—even evil needs—they didn't create and could never legitimately satisfy* (p. 57).

Clearly, you can see that Amnon was an out of control spoiled brat. He was a member of a family system that was also infected with a grandiose sense of entitlement. Entitlement may seem common within privileged families and individuals, however, it can also be found on all levels of society. So when Jonadab said to Amnon, "What's the trouble? Why should the son of a king look so dejected morning after morning?" (v. 4), you should not be surprised by Amnon's response: "I am in love with Tamar, my brother Absalom's sister." In love, he was not, in lust he most definitely was. Therefore, if you believe Amnon was in love with Tamar and wanted to do right by her, then his deception lives on. The saying goes: "If it is, it ain't." Translation: Don't be fooled by what it looks like, buy into what it does.

Chapter Three:

Rope-A-Dope Style

[5] "Well," Jonadab said, "I'll tell you what to do. Go back to bed and pretend you are ill. When your father comes to see you, ask him to let Tamar come and prepare some food for you. Tell him you'll feel better if she prepares it as you watch and feeds you with her own hands."

[6] So Amnon lay down and pretended to be sick. And when the king came to see him, Amnon asked him, "Please let my sister Tamar come and cook my favorite dish as I watch. Then I can eat it from her own hands." [7] So David agreed and sent Tamar to Amnon's house to prepare some food for him.

<u>Preying on them and not praying for them</u>

I believe I first heard the phrase "Rope-A-Dope" when boxing legend, Muhammad Ali—for whom I was named after because he was my mother's all-time favorite boxer—used it. Ali would get his opponent up against the ropes, and then pound them. Before he could do this, Ali had to set his opponent up using cunning strategies. This is important to grasp because when a person wants to obtain something or achieve a goal, they move with precision—yes, even if it is for ill gains. Ali chose to work his strategy by garnering his own strength to beat his opponent. Amnon, on the other hand, chose manipulation to conquer his prize, Tamar. Rather than earning her love in a way that would have brought honor to Tamar, Amnon plotted to violate her; thereby dishonoring her and himself as well. To make matters worse, he recruited others into his maniacal scheme—his cousin and friend, Jonadab, and his own father, King David.

Is it not possible for Amnon not to have known that Jonadab would "talk" him into tricking King David into sending Tamar to his house? I do not believe this was the case because Amnon knew what Jonadab was capable of. After all, Jonadab was his cousin and his friend. King David, on the other hand, gave into Amnon's request without questioning his intent and sent Tamar to Amnon's home to cook and care for him. Tracy (2005) wrote, "Unfortunately for Tamar, she ends up a pawn in a family power play... It also tells us something important about abusive families: *The needs of individual family members are highly expendable.* The weak members of a family can be used up and exploited to feed the appetites of the more powerful family members" (p. 56—emphasis mine).

Here is where the plot thickens. Verse 5 reads as followed: "'Well,' Jonadab said, 'I'll tell you what to do. Go back to bed and pretend you are ill. When your father comes to see you, ask him to let Tamar come and prepare some food for you. Tell him you'll feel better if she prepares it as you watch and feeds you with her own hands.'" Confidence men and women (Con men and women), or grifters, learn from and feed off each other. That's why I said Amnon knew what he was doing when he whined to Jonadab.

Amnon counted on Jonadab's cunning mind to come up with a plan to help him get what he wanted—Tamar. Had Amnon not been so hell-bent on his lascivious desires for her, he would have gotten over his carnal feelings for Tamar. Tracy (2005) said it greatly when he wrote:

> Amnon's lust might have eventually died out were it not for his interaction with his shrewd advisor, Jonadab, who had asked about his downcast countenance. Amnon told he had been depressed because he was in love with the sister of his brother. The fact that Amnon did not identify Tamar as his own sister might well suggest he had already begun to impersonalize Tamar and his familial relationship with her to justify his lust. In a healthy family, Jonadab would have corrected Amnon and coached him in the proper way to meet his relational and sexual needs. Instead, Jonadab concocted a devious scheme for Amnon to gain physical access to his sister by pretending to be ill and calling for his sister to feed him (verses 3 – 5). Jonadab was Amnon's cousin, and as a member of the family he should have been concerned for Tamar's welfare and his cousin's moral well-being (pp. 57 – 58).

My educated guess as to why Jonadab wanted to help Amnon was because he wanted to satisfy his cousin's wicked urges to win favor in Amnon's sight. In my opinion, they viewed Tamar as a thing, an object that would quench Amnon's sexual thirst for the moment. Their actions were similar to a mother, who was violated in her lifetime, carrying the "she'll be alright" attitude toward her daughter, when the mother is well aware of a potentially harmful situation her child may face. Looking at the quote I used from Stone's (2004) work in the previous chapter—parents should know what creates pain in their child's life (I paraphrase). The daughter's desire to receive the admiration of an older male for whom she holds in high esteem, may have been her goal. But little does this child know, this man might not be the one she needs to receive attention from. Let's see what else Stone (2004) has to say about the attention seeking behavior or the looking for love phenomena as it relates to abuse:

> Maybe our kids are so hungry for nurturing that abuse looks like love to them. Maybe we're not talking and listening to them enough. Maybe some adult is paying too much attention to them and parents are too preoccupied to see the warning signs. If abuse is not properly addressed and treated, it can sow the seeds of further dysfunction. The secrets and lies keep us from developing and nurturing open relationships with one another, and keep abuse survivors from living fully. Families come to know one another—and the world—through a veil of deception (pp. 18 – 19).

Allow me to digress for a moment and explain why I do not like the labels such as *victims* and *survivors*, especially when it comes to sexual abuse. When a person experiences trauma such as sexual assault, there is a great deal of shame attached to that occurrence. When a person, who had been raped, is labeled a rape victim or a rape survivor, they are in essence, reconnected to that shame-filled experience in their life again. In other words, they are revictimized all over again. This is not to say people purposely set out to do so, but the implications that are attached to such labels may strike an injurious chord unintentionally. When I hear the words victim and survivor, my mind asks the question: Of what? Personally, I would rather hear something more up-lifting, more liberating, and more empowering. I am not suggesting that we forget about our pasts because our life's story is our testimony. What I am suggesting is that we use phrases that will empower people whom had to endure and survive horrific episodes in their lives. How about conquerors or overcomers?

* * * * *

Amnon and Jonadab were two of the worst kinds of thieves and violators known to human-kind because they counted on Tamar's loyalty to the king to manipulate her. Verses 6 and 7 reads:

> So Amnon lay down and pretended to be sick. And when the king came to see him, Amnon asked him, "Please let my sister Tamar come and cook my favorite dish as I watch. Then I can eat it from her own hands." So David agreed and sent Tamar to Amnon's house to prepare some food for him.

Wow! If I were King David or in a situation like this, I would have questions regarding Amnon's request, especially when comes down to my daughter, my sister, and young girls I know or in general. Again, a weaker, insignificant, expendable member of the family, Tamar was sent in to satisfy the stronger member's hankerings. King David reinforced Amnon's self-absorbed proclivities by agreeing to send someone he should have held in high esteem, one he should have been more inclined to protect—his precious daughter, Tamar. King David's abhorrent decision, which could have been rooted in his own guilt and shame from his past transgressions, impacted the lives of many of his own children through death, division, and ultimately, a civil war. Tracy (2005) addressed King David's behavior in the ensuing manner: "David fully cooperated with Amnon's fiendish plan, ordering Tamar to go to Amnon's house and prepare him food" (p. 58). This decision was a tradeoff between King David's powerful and vulnerable offspring. However, Tracy's words continued to cut like a knife when he asserted:

> If this was all the information we had regarding David's response to Tamar, we might conclude he had been so thoroughly deceived that he bore little responsibility for the violation of Tamar. David's pattern of behavior toward his children shows otherwise. In fact, David demonstrates another trait of abusive families: *Vulnerable family members are not protected because no one really wants to know the truth* (pp. 58 – 59, emphasis mine).

Doesn't this make your blood boil? David showed what we call today, favoritism. Favoritism gives special preference to one child over the other, but this went far beyond favoritism. What King David did was parallel to bartering livestock in order to keep his heir-apparent happy, but it was Tamar who would pay the greatest price in the end.

Is It Worth It?

The sense of belonging is a human trait that most of us have. To be denied this connectedness creates a deep-seated longing that will remain until it is satisfied; regardless if it is conductive to our well-being or not. In fact, some people would go to any length to be attached to others to their own detriment. In King David's family, there was an urgent need for connectedness that caused a lot of collateral damage amongst his children and extended family, especially his daughter, Tamar. If the members of this royal family were honest with themselves, they would have admitted that they had problems in their lives, and their problems spilled over onto one another. Kaufman (1992) wrote that "Identification begins within the family" (p. 38). Unfortunately, Tamar's identification was shaped within a system that was deeply flawed in that it embodied personalities who were reckless, for a lack of better words. Kaufman further explained this occurrence by saying:

Learning how to become a person originates through identification, as we first identify and thereby have a beginning base from which to navigate the human world. This idea is pivotal to all that follows. Only

40

later do we individuate [come into our own] by differentiating our own unique self. These two processes, identification and differentiation, alternate with one another as we go about the task of becoming a fully separate person. ...Phenomenologically, identification involves a merging with another, a partial giving up, if only for a brief moment, of one's separate self (p. 38).

Therefore, in King David's family system, his children were born into an established dynamic whereby they learned and took their places within that system. Systemically speaking, the family members were actualizing or fulfilling what they had been exposed to from those around them. Yet this is not an excuse for the parents to acquiesce in their parental duties in that they do not take on their needed roles in their children's lives. Kaufman (1992) clarified the parents' role within the family system in terms of the child searching for and achieving his or her individuality when he wrote:

Modeling of parental behavior is one vehicle for identification, but alone, it is not sufficient. Most especially it is through open and close *communication* between parent and child that the much-needed experience of identification takes place. And the parent must *permit* the child to identify with him or her in order for positive identification to occur. Talking with a child about what is truly important to the parent... is what enables the child to join either parent experientially through the child's own imagery

41

and, in so doing, to feel identified with or a part of that parent. In this way the child learns about the parent from the inside, learns what is like almost to be that other human being who is so important to the child. In a most significant way such an experience of identification at critical times provides need support, strength, and healing for an evolving self (p. 39).

Whenever a person proclaims: "I got it honestly" it is usually pointing to a behavior or a way of life that the individual feels is faulty or not too positive. Many people trained in counseling or psychology would call this occurrence enmeshed, entangled, or embedded. I would refer to all of them at different times and situations. I chose to use embedded in regards to King David's family system, and I looked to Lewis' (1995) discussion of being embedded to help corroborate my perspective on this matter:

The embeddedness of individuals within their social and natural context can occur whether the context is a fixed entity or a changing pattern of action. In a changing pattern of action and role, the self assumes many different forms; in a fixed pattern, the self may not. Even so, in both types of context, the self is embedded in other we-selves and is defined by these we-selves (p. 214).

To be embedded, in this sense, is to be unable to see or do something different from the rest of the people within the group and/or family. Therefore, the chances of rocking the boat within that environment could be slim to none. And so it was within King David's family system.

In this story, it seemed to be an unspoken code of loyalty where King David's family members were expected to be faithful to the king, to their country, to their villages or their neighbors, and to their family—at least to some of their family members. They were expected to uphold themselves in a certain manner, and this was the case in the story of Tamar. She was required to be obedient onto the king and to follow his commands. Tamar understood there were ramifications for defying the king and her brothers, especially if they had favor with the king. These expectations stood out in the lives of the king's children and the people he ruled over. We all live with certain expectations in our lives. Sometimes we live up to them, and other times we do not. In fact, Diederich (2006) described expectations in the following fashion:

> We all live with expectations for the way our lives SHOULD be. There are expectations that people have *for us*—like our family or teachers. Then there are expectations that *God* has for us—or, at least the expectations we *think* God has for us. Plus, there are the expectations that we have for ourselves. That is a lot of expectations!

Many of these expectations we live up to, but unfortunately, we also fall short of many of them. Falling short is part of the human condition… We all fall short, but for most of us, falling short doesn't feel very good and that is **where shame comes in**… If you are a well adjusted person, falling short of expectations may not affect you very much at all. Either you realize that you set your expectations too high and so you lower them or you simply decide to work a little harder to achieve your goals—no big deal. But for some of us, it is not that simple. Falling short of our life expectations can be devastating. We see it as a statement of our value… (pp. 9, 10, bold emphasis mine).

If expectations are not viewed and/or approached in a healthy way, they can be overwhelming and stressful. Oftentimes we do not meet them or other people do not uphold those standards we place on them. I learned a valuable lesson about expectations when I was parenting my younger sister some years ago. Sometimes we, as parents and older members in our families and communities, place visions of grandeur and high standards on our children, and expect them to live up to them without question or protest. We enforce a "my way or the highway" mentality on them, which causes our children much consternation. We expect or demand them to obey and pursue what we feel is right for them. But what we do not anticipate is this may cause the child or person to feel as if they do not measure up to our demands when they are not achieved. However, there is one very important reality we must grasp here: Our expectations may not match our children's expectations and goals for themselves, which leads to conflicts. The result of these clashes can be seen when a child comes of age, they leave their parents' home and do not return or when they do return look these visits are very brief. This might derive from the parents living vicariously through their children. Sorenson (2006) explained it this way:

> Parents are often so focused on what they want for their children, who they want their children to be, and what they want their children to accomplish that they ignore the individual traits, needs, and abilities of each child. Without realizing it, they may push their children in ways that fulfill their own desires and dreams while totally disregarding the aspirations of their children and the right of those children to live their own dreams and set their own goals. Unaware they are doing so, parents often us their children in this way to assuage their own pain over mistakes made or opportunities lost. Unhappy with their own lives and choices, they try to compensate by taking charge of the lives of their children, as though they get to use these lives as a second chance. They give unsolicited, attempting to steer their children into futures that match their own preferences, not considering that the child may have totally different goals in life (p. 220).

I also like the way Stone (2004) talked about being a part of a family and belonging when she wrote the ensuing words:

Most of us take for granted the requirements for belonging to a family, if we've given it any thought at all. Perhaps if we had to sign a contract we'd be forced to acknowledge the awesome responsibilities that come with being a part of a clan.… Every family has an unspoken trust. It's the assumption that kin should be a source of nurturing, sharing, and safety. Unfortunately, not all of our families provide all of these things, but each family member at least has a responsibility to keep its children safe… (p. 17).

Tamar was let her down in ways I am sure she had never imagined. She was betrayed by her brother, her cousin and her father. Sadly, this is a harsh reality for far too many people. We look to our family for a certain degree of security and protection by way of helping us as we develop through the impartation of wisdom and helping us to navigate through life and situations we should avoid. When we are left to fend for ourselves, like the daughter whose mother's attitude toward her was "she'll be alright," we come to feel bitter about our family or even loath them for deserting us in our time of need.

I can imagine Tamar replaying the fact that her very own father sent her to Amnon's house without diligently checking into what he was really up to. King David failed Tamar in the most atrocious way a father can fail his daughter. Here is how Tracy (2005) talked about this family's dynamics and King David's dereliction of his parental (and spiritual) duties when he wrote:

46

The truth is ignored. In other words, maintaining one's own emotional well-being is more important than admitting that dangerous family problems exist. As the God-ordained spiritual leader charged with the well-being of his household, David should have known, at the very least, that something was wrong with Amnon, whose depression was quite evident to other family members. The fact that Amnon was next in line to the throne made it even more inexcusable that David failed to observe such wholesale moral turmoil in his own son. Amnon's moral character most likely had been eroding over an extended period of time. No spiritually healthy man wakes up one morning and secedes he's going to rape his sister. David apparently chose to see nothing and do nothing, and Tamar was eventually raped as a result (p. 59).

Many times, people choose to ignore what is real. This is a disparaging fact. Sometimes people *choose* not to see things as they really are. Case and point, there are times when a person can see a problem arising, and know how damaging the affects could be on a person; but he or she might create space between themselves and the other person—"Out of sight, out of mind." With this created space, the first person can easily and truthfully say, "I didn't see anything." Initially, one can believe this explanation has some legitimacy because the person was not there and, therefore, could not have possibly witnessed what transpired. That's fine and very well may be what it appears to be; however, it is my contention that if he or she had an inkling of what the outcome could have been based on his or her experience and/or knowledge derived from their intuitive insight—we call this spiritual

47

insight—then, they should bear some degree of responsibility for not doing something to help the other person. As quoted above, Tracy (2005) points to the fact that "As the God-ordained spiritual leader charged with the well-being of his [her] household" or whatever the person's capacity is, he or she "should have known, at the very least, that something was wrong" or was going awry. Yet, instead, he or she "apparently chose to see nothing and do nothing," (Tracey, 2005, p. 59).

To be sure, this is one the most egregious forms of denial, which can also be seen as neglect, that a person could carry out. It is an offense to humanity and a sin before God. Some people are quick to say, "It's none of my business, anyway." Again, that may very well be true. You do have the right to choose not to do or say anything—I don't know how you sleep at night or look at yourself in the mirror—but at some point, you must ask yourself: Is what I'm doing or not doing right? One of my past mentors used to say to me a lot: "If you have a question, the answer is in that question." Any person with an average conscience would feel uncomfortable with the decision to not to do anything. But, one whom has made the choice not to do anything may be protecting themselves. From the outside looking in on this type of situation, we can easily judge and condemn that person for not doing something to help; but we do not know that person's heart or their story. What we do not know about that person might be the very thing that may be tearing his or her emotional/psychological world apart. Unbeknownst to us, this person might be struggling with the same or a similar situation unfolding before their eyes. For whatever reason, King David acted as if he did not notice Amnon's downward moral and spiritual spiral into decadence and carnality. Therefore, Tamar was deprived of needed protection.

Chapter Four:

The Lowering of the Boom

[8] When Tamar arrived at Amnon's house, she went to the place where he was lying down so he could watch her mix some dough. Then she baked his favorite dish for him. [9] But when she set the serving tray before him, he refused to eat. "Everyone get out of here," Amnon told his servants. So they all left.

[10] Then he said to Tamar, "Now bring the food into my bedroom and feed it to me here." So Tamar took his favorite dish to him.

In the last chapter, I talked about expectations, being protected by those who are charged with caring for us, and ensuring that our well being is guarded and promoted. I also briefly discussed the lapse in this protection. At this point in the Tamarry's, you saw that she was obediently doing as her father, King David, commanded her to do—go to Amnon's house to cook and care for him because he was ill. However, it is time to take a closer look at this story.

This portion of Tamar's story tells us that Amnon was in position to carry out his wicked plan to take advantage of her. As Tamar was preparing the meal for Amnon, he saw this act as a titillating dance, if you will, and his wicked desires stir more and more. When Tamar finished cooking and baking for Amnon, he would not eat because his appetite was not for food. His voracious hunger was for Tamar's body. He could not wait to be alone with her, so he broke what was probably not customary in his house and sent all of his servants away. They obediently did as Amnon commanded and went away. You see Amnon abused his influence to get what he wanted, and his servants probably did not want to rock the boat or upset him by staying. Amnon's position over his servants carried two types of weight: He was their boss and he was a prince whose family ruled over the land in which they lived. Therefore, the servants probably feared Amnon and did not want to receive the wrath of a mad man. Tracy (2005) wrote, "Amnon's ruse worked, and after sending the servants away, he gained private access to Tamar" (p. 60). And what does Amnon do with this exclusive access to Tamar? He perpetrates some of the foulest acts against Tamar that one can carry out toward humanity—he abused her in a variety of ways.

Amnon's next power play was to get Tamar to come closer by commanding, "Now bring the food into my bedroom and feed it to me here." So Tamar took the dish to him (v. 10a). Tamar, not thinking anything of it, did as her brother requested—she came closer to Amnon to feed him (v. 10b). Amnon presented as a person too sick to care for himself, let alone feed himself. As Tamar dutifully fulfills the purpose of her visit and the wishes of her father, the king, Amnon makes his move. The Bible says "he grabbed her and demanded, 'Come to bed with me, my darling sister'" (v. 11). Tracy (2005) described this scene by saying:

At this point he wasted no more time pretending to be a bedridden invalid. He grabbed Tamar and lewdly demanded sex. The language of the text highlights Amnon's abusive use of physical force to hold Tamar against her will... Amnon's demand was both crass and confusing; for this was the first and only time he called Tamar "my sister" (2 Samuel 13:11)... abusers manipulate with their words and actions and have little regard for the impact of their manipulation on the victim. For Tamar, "sister" should have been a term denoting a tender familial relationship that elicited steadfast loyalty, care, and protection. Instead, this sister received violent defilement, contempt, and abandonment (p. 60).

Amnon's acts of trickery and exploitation toward the people around him culminated during his time alone with Tamar. You see, Amnon took this opportunity to try to convince Tamar to lay with him, believing she would willingly have sex with him. It had to be his own hubris (exaggerated pride in one's self) that convinced him that Tamar would not resist his advances. If you recall from the previous chapter, Tamar was viewed as a dispensable, irrelevant object, there for Amnon's use. This was validated when Jonadab devised a plan to convince King David to send Tamar to Amnon's house to ease his wonton desires, and King David granted Amnon's request without inquisition or scrutiny. In essence, Tamar was set up for the Ookie-doke, where she would find herself in a precarious position with nowhere to go or no one to turn to in order to get out of this predicament.

Unfortunately, Amnon's lewd demand for sex from Tamar was not the end of this disturbing scene. As I go forward in this story, you will see different forms of abuse Amnon leveled against Tamar emerge. I am quite sure she was probably still reeling from the shock of being asked for sex from a brother she most likely held in high regard. This may be akin to people believing that their investments were solid and profitable with a trusted friend or firm only to find that every penny they put into it was gone. Gut-wrenching! This was Tamar's position: She was in a place where the other person made his true intentions known and they were not in her favor.

Weakened and Ashamed

Other forms of abuse should be clear by now—bullying and intimidation. Notice how Amnon spoke to Tamar. Verse 10 says, after Tamar finished cooking his meal, Amnon said, "Now bring the food into my bedroom and feed it to me here." I cannot imagine this request being made in an inviting fashion. In my estimation, Amnon knew Tamar well enough to know she would not refuse his request because she wanted to please her "sick" brother. Amnon was sick all right. He was set in his reprobate mind! People who bully or use intimidation to get what he or she wants from other people may have been victims of the same tactics at some point of their lives. Yes, I get that people would say that's just their personality or "the way I am," but.... Some people believe their behaviors are "normal," and they should be accepted as them being who they are, but my moral scope tells me there is something wrong when a person's behavior hurts another person. However, the "normal" folk tend to view parties whom are different from them as strange, weird, and other derogatory adjectives. Goffman (1963), in his classic work entitled *Stigma*, described this group as "stigmatized" individuals. This kind of degradation can and will have injurious effects on those whom are/were bullied and/or stigmatized. Let's look at what Goffman wrote when the two groups—the "normals" and the stigmatized—occupy the same space:

> The very anticipation of such contacts can of course lead normals and stigmatized to arrange life so as to avoid them. Presumably this will have larger consequences for the stigmatized, since more arranging will usually be necessary on their part... Lack the salutary feed-back of daily social intercourse with others, the self-isolate can become suspicious, depressed, hostile, anxious, and bewildered... When normals and stigmatized do in fact enter one another's immediate presence, especially when they attempt to sustain a joint conversational encounter, there occurs one of the primal scenes of sociology; for, in many cases, these moments will be the ones when the causes and effects of stigma must be directly confronted. The stigmatized individual may find that he [or she] feels unsure of how we normals will identify him [or her] and receive him [or her] (pp. 12, 13).

This occurs when people like Tamar (the stigmatized) dwell in a space with people like Amnon (the "normals"). The stigmatized individuals will probably feel awkward and uncertain if they might fall prey to the "normals" in this situation, rather than being comfortable with being who they really are. When the stigmatized individual experiences belittlement, being berated, and battered—either physically or emotionally—their defective foundation is reinforced as their faulty sense of self is further compromised. At this point, he or she will receive affirmations as to their devalued self, whether real or imagined, from those around them. The stigmatized person, then, behaves as they were taught by those around them. However, idealistically, we should want to see our loved ones and/or others thrive emotionally, mentally, as well as socially. Kaufman and Raphael (1991) wrote, "If developing a conscious, competent self challenges our confidence, skill, and determination, establishing satisfying human relationships presents no less a challenge" (p. 95). One way to further challenge the development of our proficient self is to not be encouraged or taught our worth. Achieving a competent self is a lifelong endeavor, which requires positive, affirming relationships that edifies and strengthen us. Kaufman and Raphael continued onto admonish us in the following passage:

> We are not born knowing how to be a competent self; neither are we born knowing how to navigate the human world. Our ability to make meaningful, if not lasting, connection with other people requires a set of skills which must be learned through practice. Having relationships is indeed a craft which must be worked at actively if it is to be learned at all... We must have free access to our affects (feelings), needs, drives, and purposes. We must be able to experience, name, and own all of the different parts of the self within us as distinguishable parts of an integrated self. We must live consciously within ourselves as well as in that outer world of people and things, seeing the reality of people and situations confronting us as objectively and honestly as possible. Matching our

expectations with reality, as we have considered this skill earlier, lies at the heart of the craft of interpersonal relating (p. 95).

These writers' perspective can be akin to the nature versus nurture debate in that if a person does not learn to be sociable in certain settings, he or she will not be able to be or feel competent in other social settings. It is not a question of a person being naturally inclined or born with certain social skills, they are taught them, and then, he or she takes to them either "naturally" or "proficiently." This is the case when a person is bullied or stigmatized. He or she will have to literally be reprogrammed or re-indoctrinated in order for their outlook and inward feelings and thoughts of themselves to change.

Tamar decided to check out on life and separated herself from others. I believe her socialization within her family-of-origin sparked her reaction long before this incident that led to Tamar withdrawing from the rest of the world. Take a look at what Goffman (1963) wrote some years ago when he discussed the socialization of stigmatized individuals:

One pattern involves those with an inborn stigma who become socialized into their disadvantageous situation even while they are learning and incorporating the standards against which they fall short... A second pattern derives from the capacity of a family, and to a much lesser extent a local neighborhood, to constitute itself a protective capsule for its young. Within such a capsule a congenitally stigmatized child can be carefully sustained by means of information control. Self-belittling definitions of him [or her] are prevented from entering the charmed circle, while broad access is given to other conceptions held in the wider society, ones that lead the encapsulated child to see himself [or herself] as a fully qualified ordinary human being, of normal identity in terms of such basic matters as age and sex... The point in the protected individual's life when the domestic circle can no longer protect him will vary by social class, place of residence, and type of stigma, but in each case will give rise to a moral experience when it occurs (pp. 32 – 33).

It is easy to say, "Shake that off," or "Take a stand against that bully." They might also be tempted to say, "Don't stand for that," when his or her environment is stigmatized as well. In other words, how can a person whom is being (or has been) bullied or is stigmatized achieve a competent self when those around them also "fall short" of the "standards" of what is deemed normal? One answer could be he or she has to be exposed to other settings outside of his or her familiar environment in order to discover a new and at times drastically different perspective as to what is available to them. This is what I believe Goffman (1963) meant by the last line of the above quotation—"The point in the protected individual's life when the domestic circle can no longer protect him will vary by social class, place of residence, and type of stigma, but in each case will give rise to a moral experience when it occurs" (p. 33).

I have had the opportunity to work with boys and

girls, both young children and adolescents, whom had been bullied. Some of them learned how to become the bully rather than being bullied; while others struggled with the residual affects (feelings) of being bullied. The most difficult challenge I have seen thus far is breaking the old habits that once protected them. For example, many people who are or have been bullied in their lifetime experience an enormous amount of shame because not only were they harassed emotionally, mentally and physically, they also discover they were "different" and/or stigmatized in the harshest way. They developed and utilized varying means of escaping and/or separating themselves from situations to which they are actually being tormented or may feel as if they are being bullied. In other words, in regards to the latter, a person may be in a place where bullying *is* active, he or she may go far into their own world—or as my sister would say, "Have a moment." Unfortunately, this type of escapism is accompanied by shutting others out when it comes to how they feel about what happened to them. This makes it unbelievably difficult to develop and/or sustain healthy, loving, trusting relationships with others.

Not only do individuals whom have felt the devastation of being stigmatized and bullied suffer, but those who love and care for them feel it too because they want to help their family or friends move past their experiences to become stronger and better people. In doing so, he or she may vacillate back and forward in their progress or shift in their mentality to the chagrin of their loved ones. "Given the ambivalence built into the individual's attachment to his [or her] stigmatized category," Goffman (1963) wrote, "it is understandable that oscillations may occur in his [or her] support of, identification with, and participation among his [or her] own" (p. 38). Those whom are attempting to help the individual climb out of this dreadful of abyss, which is sometimes called the victim's mentality, can also feel a variety of emotions. Frustration, fear and anger can and will develop as he or she continues to fluctuate between the victim and victor statuses. I can relate to both groups in that I had been bullied when I was a child, and I am currently assisting a teen who presents as a "tough cookie to break." I find myself oscillating between feelings as they go from empowered to helpless—I feel frustrated, fearful, impatience, angry, the whole gamut—because the cookie is not ready to crumble, even if the emotional fall-out becomes increasingly overwhelming for them. Irritation comes because of the obviousness of the issues as evidenced by their behaviors and emotionality; the dread appears when the threat of hopelessness is seen; and irritation when they shut-down emotionally. Goffman expounded on the thought of him or her moving back and forward when he wrote:

> There will be "affiliation cycles" through which he comes to accept the special opportunities for in-group participation or comes to reject them after having accepted them before. There will be corresponding oscillations in belief about the nature of own group and the nature of normals.... The relationship of the stigmatized individual to the informal community and formal organization of his own kind is, then, crucial. This relationship will, for example, mark a great difference between those whose differences provide them very little of a new "we," and those, such as minority group members, who find themselves a part of a well-organized community with the longstanding traditions—a community that makes appreciable claims on loyalty and income, defining the member as

someone who should take pride in his illness and not seek to get well. In any case, whether the stigmatized group is an established one or not, it's largely in relation to this own-group that it is possible to discuss the natural history and the moral career of the stigmatized individual (1963, p. 38).

What I believe the author was saying is, even though tough cookie may not be a victim of a bully currently, he or she has more to deal with apart from being bullied in the past. If a transformation is to be effectively achieved, one has to consider how and/or where the stigma came from. In other words, there is a source from which a person became stigmatized to begin with. Therefore, as I have come to realize, a great deal of patience, love and continuous affirmations must be implored in order for tough cookie to break the cycle of moving back and forth between "affiliation cycles." Compassionate, positive, unwavering presence will prove to be crucial in tough cookie's life once he or she reaches a turning point in their life.

Part Two:

When Love Turns

Into Pain

Chapter Five:

Calling It What It Is—Violation

[11] But as she was feeding him, he grabbed her and demanded, "Come to bed with me, my darling sister." [12] "No, my brother!" she cried. "Don't be foolish! Don't do this to me! Such wicked things aren't done in Israel. [13] Where could I go in my shame? And you would be called one of the greatest fools in Israel. Please, just speak to the king about it, and he will let you marry me."

[14] But Amnon wouldn't listen to her, and since he was stronger than she was, he raped her. [15] Then suddenly Amnon's love turned to hate, and he hated her even more than he had loved her. "Get out of here!" he snarled at her. [16] "No, no!" Tamar cried. "Sending me away now is worse than what you've already done to me." But Amnon wouldn't listen to her. [17] He shouted for his servant and demanded, "Throw this woman out, and lock the door behind her!"

Defying Boundaries

I want to take some time to discuss violation in a broader scope. In the above passage, the exchange between Amnon and Tamar contains a number of violations he committed against her. Certainly, the raping of Tamar was obviously an atrocious violation Amnon carried out, but there were other, more subtle, invasions of her personhood.

Turning to how one writer described violation and defined invasion, Jamal (2011) wrote:

> Being forcibly subjected to the passion of another without understanding or inviting the engagement is very difficult to process... The definition for invasion includes: any entry into an area not previously occupied. (Pathology) the spread of pathogenic microorganisms or malignant cells to new sites in the body; "the tumor's invasion of surrounding structures." I feel that a young innocent body [or anybody] that is fondled or manipulated by an adult [or anybody] has been invaded by a lustful and controlling perpetrator... The invader usurps the child's [or a person's] ability to choose a preferred time for shedding the gift of virginity [or the gift of their body]. This sacred gift is stolen, mishandled and abused (pp. 11, 13, inserts mine).

One critical mistake that is made so often is that if the perpetrator only uses words in subtle, non-abrasive ways, there was no abuse committed. Let us refer to the first sentence of the above quote for a moment to see how these so-called non-abrasive words and/or phrases a perpetrator or abuser uses to subject another person to their passion. In many social settings, it is inappropriate to tell lewd jokes. If a person is not aware of or disregards this unspoken rule, they may remain quiet or will not tell that person that their words made them feel uncomfortable. In a sense, the person telling the joke is using force on the person whom feels uncomfortable. When coupled with the definition of invasion, our joker enters a region of the other person's mind that they had not previously occupied nor was invited into willingly by the other person.

Another way in which invasion is achieved; whether it is intentionally or not is by the person who is in control or in a position of authority usurping or seizing the other person's ability to choose. You can see this when a person says, "You're going to do this whether you like it or not." Depending on the context and/or what "this" is, the person for whom this statement addresses may be forced to endure violation and abuse. In the case of Tamar and Amnon, he not only made a vulgar demand of Tamar, but he grabbed her. Verse eleven says, "But as she [Tamar] was feeding him, he *grabbed* her and demanded, 'Come to bed with me, my darling sister'." Amnon's actions and words was blatant abuse of his position over Tamar because he used intimidation to force her to acquiesce to his insidious request. Apparently, this was not in Tamar's plan or what she wanted because she invoked the cardinal declaration when she said "No, my brother!" (v. 12a). Again, referring to the quote listed above, "The invader usurps the child's [or the person's] ability to choose a preferred time for shedding the gift of virginity [or the gift of their body] (Jamal, 2011, p. 13). Amnon had already made up his mind that he would take what he wanted; however, he used persuasive seduction first, in hopes that Tamar would give in. Tamar declined Amnon's advances and he forced himself on her anyhow.

Sensing this situation was not going very well for her, Tamar pleaded with her brother by saying, "'No, my brother!' she cried. 'Don't be foolish! Don't do this to me! Such wicked things aren't done in Israel. Where could I go in my shame? And you would be called one of the greatest fools in Israel. Please, just speak to the king about it, and he will let you marry me'" (vv. 12 -13). You see, Tamar referred to shame. The shame she was speaking of was if Amnon took her virginity outside of marriage, she would be viewed as tainted and not pure; thereby, making it hard for her to be able to marry honorably. She would wear this shame for the rest of her life. But, Amnon being so self-centered and degenerate, none of this mattered to him. He wanted what he wanted—Tamar's body. Tracy (2005) explained this scene in the following way:

> After Amnon's brash proposition, Tamar had the inner strength to offer a courageous response. The clarity and logic of her response make her rape all the more tragic. While being held against her will, she immediately spoke up and gave Amnon three 'don'ts" in 2 Samuel 13: 12 (don't violate me; don't do what isn't done in Israel; don't do such a disgraceful thing) and three "ands" in verse 13 (and it would disgrace me so that I'd have to get rid of my reproach somehow; and you will become a public fool; and the king won't deny your request if you ask him for my hand in marriage)…

> Tamar's response was logical, wise, and in harmony with God's standards. But her story teaches us this sad reality when it comes to abuse situations: *The victim's response is often futile.* The tragedy here is that when abuse victims rise above the swirling waves of distorted and hurtful verbal messages and gather the courage to speak the truth, their words often fall on deaf ears. Abusers rarely respond to reason, which is why it's vital for families and churches to focus on listening to, empowering, and protecting abuse victims" (p. 61).

I agree with Tracy in the sense that logic does not work when a person tries to appeal to the predator's moral compass, when the predator is not utilizing logic or moral compass in the first place. However, it is an all-together different situation when the person whom was violated by someone whom was supposed to listen to, empower, and protect them. That was Tamar's situation: *her own family repeatedly violated and disappointed her.* In a desperate attempt to avoid being invaded by Amnon, Tamar tried to appeal to Amnon's sensibilities by encouraging him to ask for her hand in marriage, and then, Amnon's desires would have been legitimated under the sanctity of matrimony. However, Amnon was too far gone under the pull of his carnal desires.

It Was Not Supposed to Be

Amnon goes on to carry out the repulsive act of raping Tamar, and setting into motion declining consequences that Tamar had to face on her own. Verse fourteen says, "But Amnon wouldn't listen to her, and since he was stronger than she was, he raped her. Then suddenly Amnon's love turned into hate, and he hated her even more than he had loved her. 'Get out of here!' he snarled at her" (v. 15). How despicable is it that a man, who had the potential to do great things, who had women throwing themselves at him, and other men wished they could be like, to force himself onto another person in such an ugly way? Instead of being honorable and gracious to such a beautiful person, Amnon did the unthinkable: He took a part of another person he was not invited to partake, Tamar's precious body. Not only did Tamar have to deal with the staggering fact that she had been raped, and raped by her own brother, but she was being disposed of in such a humiliating fashion. The question is: What happened to Amnon sense of right and wrong? Why did Amnon want Tamar out of his presence? After all, she was willing to stay with him, even though he sullied her in a horrific way? One answer could be that he was done with her and wanted to dispose of her like a piece of trash (I had to breathe on this one). Amnon's brutal actions and nauseating sentiments toward Tamar should cause one to feel uneasy, empathize with Tamar, and possibly feel a sense of disdain toward Amnon, and people like him.

Before moving onto the next chapter let's look at verses sixteen and seventeen: "'No, no!' Tamar cried. 'Sending me away now is worse than what you've already done to me.' But Amnon wouldn't listen to her. He shouted for his servant and demanded, 'Throw this woman out, and lock the door behind her!'" In essence, Tamar was degraded and dishonored for an incident to which she lost control of. She was treated with scorn by the one who violated her to begin with! What impudence shown by Amnon that he would turn her away in such a manner as if she had committed a crime against him! Tracy (2005) wrote, "Tragically, Amnon's abusive behavior did not stop with the rape. After his lust was satiated, hate welled up in his heart, and he ordered Tamar to 'get up, go away!'" (p. 65). In my opinion, the act of putting Tamar out of his home was not about her at all. It had more to do with Amnon's guilt and shame over what he had done *to* Tamar. For Tamar to refuse to leave after having her virginity ripped away in such a horrible way shows that she still had hope for this situation. In the end, she wanted to preserve herself in a way that would have shielded her from future shame. Tracy went on to write:

Tamar refused to leave, arguing that to send her away was more evil than the rape itself. Amnon's response was to order the servants to "throw this woman out" and bolt the door...

While it seems very strange to modern readers that a woman would want to stay with her rapist, we must put Tamar's actions in their historical context. In an ancient patriarchal culture that placed great emphasis on sexual purity and honor, a young woman who had lost her virginity, even through rape, would few chances of marriage. Without marriage, a woman would have little chance of supporting herself and thus leave her with no social and financial future. *She would also be unable to have children, which was the single most important role of women in Jewish culture.... Thus, Tamar cried out that Amnon's second act was a greater wrong than the first, for in kicking her out and not marrying her, he was killing her future...* Amnon thus showed great disdain for Tamar by declaring, in essence, that she wasn't worthy to be married to *anyone*, not even to her rapist... (p. 65, emphasis mine).

My God! Talk about being violated only to be violated again! This was not the way it was supposed to be. Tamar deserved a choice, she deserved a future. Yet Amnon did not see it that way. He ignored all of this when he pursued Tamar, defiled her, and discarded her. Tamar felt desperately trapped and demonstrated what we might say were symptoms of Stockholm Syndrome today, by begging

Ammnon not to push her out and her refusal to leave.

Chapter Six:

All Is Not Gone

[18] So the servant put her out and locked the door behind her. She was wearing a long, beautiful robe, as was the custom in those days for the king's virgin daughters. [19] But now Tamar tore her robe and put ashes on her head. And then, with her face in her hands, she went away crying.

Just Because You Are

We have reached the most challenging portion of this writing process. Like the person who delivers the message during a preaching moment, this process was designed to move me along in life, as well as others. In order to be true to this process, I must admit that I continue to struggle with moving forward, even though my past is in the past. I am cognizant of the fact that I am not the only person in the world tussling with "issues." I am a human being who is beleaguered with a sundry of things at different times in my life. Therefore, I believe it would be more effective for the reader if I shared a little bit about my own experiences in this forum. My former pastor, the late Reverend John D. Coleman, told me: "Book knowledge is a wonderful thing, but experience is more respectable."

I have discovered a crucial truth in the therapeutic process that proves to be very productive: When a person arrives at a place where he or she is able to truly engage in self-disclosure, he or she is ready to allow healing to take place in their lives. What this means is *the* person is comfortable, mentally and emotionally prepared, and he or she is willing and able to talk about various areas of their lives freely, in a safe environment, of course. Something within him or her is ready to release feelings that are the result of a traumatic event in his or her life. Their disclosure can include their joys, their sorrows, their difficulties, their triumphs and their defeats. These areas are all a part of life, and we all will experience them as we live.

As for me, many people who know me, personally or socially, will say I have accomplished many things in my life, and that is true. It has been a wonderful ride so far, and I do appreciate the depth of all that God has brought me through. However, there are some things in my life I have yet to face, let alone overcome—true intimacy. At this point in my life, one of my desires is to find a woman who is fitting to be my wife, my friend, my lover, my sounding board, my confidant, and my soul mate. Many people, especially those I encounter regularly, scratch their heads in wonderment because this has not happened yet. From the outset the answer may appear to be simple—"You have to get out there and mingle to find her." The truth of the matter is that it not so simple for me because I had not dealt with, walked through a situation that occurred in my life. The situation that has negatively affected my life is that I had to endure being sexually assaulted by a woman I trusted. I did not have a reason to believe she would do such a grotesque thing that violated me because she was "horny." In some ways, I tried to convince myself that I should have laid back and enjoyed it—that is if I functioned out of the macho male ego or in the same demented mind-set as she. But that was not where my head was, nor was she someone I thought of in that way.

I struggled for many years following this episode because I felt that I deserved being treated that way, because of my past behaviors up to that point in my life. I felt that this person treated me the way I treated myself and others, in a sense. I did not always treat myself with respect nor did I always love myself for who I was at that time. Although I have never been considered suicidal, but there were times when I questioned and "demanded" God to "take me home." I had never tried to harm myself, but I did feel like I was like "scum" at times and like I did not deserve too much out of life. As crazy as it may seem right now, I did not truly understand the concept of people deserving respect, or that we all have a right to maintain some level of dignity in our lives, regardless of what we say or do. I thought I should have been treated that way because I did not feel worthy of anything other than being a "piece," a thing, an object. I thought and felt I was reaping what I had sewn. But that did not make sense because I had *never* violated anyone like that in my life. Realizing this helped me to understand and pursue healing and change in my life.

Thank goodness God had a plan for my life. Since then, I have engaged in therapy and have had a number of positive relationships with people who genuinely love me and care enough about me to affirm me. The interesting thing about these encouraging relationships is that these individuals do not cater to my ego by codling me, telling me things I want to hear, or sparing my feelings. Oh no! There are times when I get the full strength of their love by being told the truth regardless of how much it hurt. Don't get me wrong, I do not enjoy giving and receiving pain, however, sometimes in order for me to grow, things must be cut out of my life. This is not always a warm and fuzzy feeling. It hurts! And I love and appreciate my friends, my brothers and sisters, for loving on me in a way that is edifying in Christ.

There are times when still I feel some of the long-term effects, even years after that violation. I still distrust intimate relationships, to a certain extent, where I feel that I am not worthy of such an experience. I know this is the devil's job—to keep me bound in this type thinking. I do want to get married someday, but what causes me consternation is that I think my "Mrs. Right" will use and abuse me in some way. Somewhere in the darkest places of my mind, I feel vulnerable and I try to protect myself by not trusting another person whom may very well be the wife that has been set aside for me. The best way to overcome this barrier may very well be processing how I feel about that situation from my past and put it in its place in my own understanding. What I must pray about is how to undo those limiting, self-defeating unconscious thoughts that bind me into thinking I am "damaged goods."

Damaged Goods

A line of questioning one could pursue if and when they observe a person whom thinks, speaks, feels, and/or

72

behaves as if they are "damaged goods" is why—"Why do they think, speak, feels and/or behave that way?" I am aware of the feelings the word "why" incites. Yes, it creates an atmosphere of an interrogation, but at some point that may very well be what is needed in order to grab their attention. However, I do not endorse this line of questioning all of the time. It is only useful in certain situations and individuals. Why questions may cause more harm than good because the person may shut down and not speak at all. Sometimes this type of questioning helps me as I engage in motivational self-talk. I don't always need to have a gentle nudge. Sometimes, the best way to get through to "this hard-headed child" is to get his or her attention. So the tough love model works for me. This approach might not have been suitable for Tamar and her situation, at first. So let's return to her story because this portion is the "driving point" of this entire book—the introduction of the source of healing that Tamar did not experience in her lifetime, or at least in Bible's account. At this point, Tamar lived her life under the crushing weight of what we call self-loathing (a form of self-hatred that may seem to be unfixable) and shame.

At this juncture of the biblical account, Amnon had tricked others, sexually assaulted Tamar, and threw her out of his home. Amnon took an audacious stance of disgust toward Tamar, although *he* was the one that tainted her in such a distasteful manner. Amnon commanded his servant to throw Tamar out, and according to the first part of verse eighteen, the servant put her out and locked the door behind her (1 Samuel 13, *NIV*).

Tamar's mental, spiritual, physical being was wounded to the point where she felt damaged and dejected, and she did not feel that she deserved to adorn the beautiful robes that were customarily worn by the royal virgin princesses. Verses 18a and 19 say, "She [Tamar] was wearing a long, beautiful robe, as was the custom in those days for the king's virgin daughters. But now Tamar tore her robe and put ashes on her head. And then, with her face in her hands, she went away crying." Tamar may have felt, like many others whom had endured such a horrific experience, as if it was *her* fault that she was a casualty of Amnon's ploy. This was Tamar's first step toward emotional self-mutilation. Self-mutilation usually refers to physically harming one's self, but any type of punishment inflected on one 's self is a form of self-mutilation. We have to keep in mind that there are polar opposites or extremes to every situation—too much or too little—that signals something is needed.

An excellent example of emotional self-mutilation can come from my own life. I have not sincerely shown an interest in dating or being intimate for a long time because "I had a lot going on in my life"—a convenient lie I had come to believe. It was partially true, but the truth of the matter was I did not want to take the risk of being hurt again. At the heart of my excuse-making mentality was I did not want to deal with my past and the feelings it created. I was not ready to see that every woman was the same as that "family friend." I denied myself of authentic intimacy by shutting that part of my life down. My distrust became an unhealthy way for me to cope. It was safer for me to bog myself down with busyness (school, work, church duties, and parenting my younger siblings) without a healthy balance of an intimate relationship. To say I stopped trying to meet someone since that horrible experience would be a stretch of the truth. I had a few relationships afterwards, including one engagement to be married at one point, but none of those relationships worked out. To some degree, I entered into them to save face of being a loner. And their devastating ends were the result of my self-sabotaging behaviors, and incompatibility to which went against something was taught as a child, not to settle for just anything.

Tamar's descend into a place of self-loathing was not a straight shot. She had help along the way. In the next chapter, we will see how significant others in Tamar's life directly affected the way she viewed herself following her traumatic ordeal. Keep in mind, a part of the shame process is being exposed or seen by others.

Chapter Seven

No Saving Face

[20] Her brother Absalom saw her and asked, "Is it true that Amnon has been with you? Well, my sister, keep quiet for now, since he's your brother. Don't you worry about it." So Tamar lived as a desolate woman in her brother Absalom's house.

[21] When King David heard what had happened, he was very angry. [22] And though Absalom never spoke to Amnon about this, he hated Amnon deeply because of what he had done to his sister.

Looking Out for Whom?

After reading the first line of this portion of Tamar's story, what question comes to mind? I immediately asked: How did Absalom know about Tamar being raped by Amnon so fast? Did he know something that Tamar should have known beforehand? It seems suspect to me because verse 20 said, "...Absalom saw her and asked...." Did he see something that led him directly to Amnon? Whatever the case, Absalom instantaneously went into "save face" and/or "damage control" mode. It is not just my suspicious mind because Tracy (2005) wrote the following to offer a balance of two perspectives:

The biblical story now shifts to Absalom, who, upon seeing Tamar's visible grief, makes several incredible statements (2 Samuel 13: 20). He first asks her if she has been with Amnon. Some interpreters take this as evidence that Absalom and Jonadab were working concert, and that Absalom had been in on the rape plan all along—which would have given him an excuse to kill Amnon so he could become heir to the throne. [Tracy's view] I believe Absalom's treatment of Tamar suggests, rather, that he loved her and had not actively conspired with her rape but had passively conspired by ignoring warnings signs of Amnon's devious intentions. *After all, abusive families aren't intimate, don't know each other well, and don't protect vulnerable family members because they don't really want to know the truth* (p. 67, emphasis mine).

When both points of view are seen in this light, I can see how both conclusions were drawn. However, since I can relate to Tamar personally, my thoughts did not sway toward the latter (the explanation) immediately. Naturally, I looked at those around Tamar. I did the same in my own situation— I looked at those who were supposed to protect me, even if I was in a drunken state, which I was frequently in during the weekends back then.

Absalom's next move was to sweep Tamar's situation under the carpet for the time being, when he told her to "keep quiet for now, since he's your brother." In other words, don't air our dirty laundry; keep this under wraps. I believe Absalom's wheels had began to turn as he became hell-bent on seeking revenge and getting rid of the next heir apparent to the throne—Amnon. Absalom, then, tried to comfort Tamar by telling her: "Don't you worry about it." Tracy (2005) described this succinctly: *"Abusive families enact a strict code of silence, especially if the abuser is a family member"* (p. 67, emphasis mine). However, this did nothing to sooth Tamar's wounded spirit because the story says, "So Tamar lived as a desolate woman in her brother Absalom's house (v. 20c). We will discuss Tamar's response—withdrawing from others and not living her life—at another time. For now, there is still some more to be said about Absalom's and David's responses and mindsets.

Verses 21 and 22 reads: "When King David heard what had happened, he was very angry. And though Absalom never spoke to Amnon about this, he hated Amnon deeply because of what he had done to his sister." Isn't it odd that the only description of King David's reaction to what happened to Tamar was he was very angry? And? According to the rest of the story, nothing else happened. King David did nothing about the brutality that was meted out upon the one who should have been just as precious to him as his heir apparent, Tamar, his daughter! Tracy (2005) presented a point of view that was more gracious than my own when he wrote:

King David's response offers a final insight into abusive families. After hearing of Tamar' rape. David was "very angry" (2 Samuel 13: 21). What is confusing is that this sovereign monarch was very angry, and yet he did absolutely nothing...David was

78

angry that Tamar was raped, but because Amnon was the firstborn golden boy, David protected him and not Tamar. Even though God's law dictated that Amnon should either be cut off from the people for committing incest (Leviticus 20: 17) or be forced to marry Tamar for raping her (Deuteronomy 22: 28-29), David insisted on protecting the abuser...." (p. 69).

Enough said! As for Absalom, my contention that he had already began the process of plotting how to exact revenge on Amnon for raping his sister, and getting rid of him so that he (Absalom) would become the heir apparent to the throne— "Absalom may well have been trying to comfort Tamar, knowing he intended to get revenge on her rapist" (Tracy, 2005, p. 68).

Who Foots the Bill?

Now that we have covered Tamar's story, how do you feel about it? Does it make you want to do something different for yourself or someone else? Have you arrived at a place where you might see these atrocities in a new light? Personally, I know it is time for me to do something drastically different, especially for our children. Although I was in my twenties when I was traumatized, I know this has to be very difficult for a child to cope with and understand. Unfortunately, the person who was violated is oftentimes left alone to deal with the effects of being sexually abused— whether it was one time or several times. The important thing for us to understand here is that the effects of abuse manifest themselves in different ways for different people. One of the responses I have heard most frequently when it is revealed that a person had been sexually violated is: "It didn't seem like anything was wrong with them." Depending upon the person's psychological/emotional makeup and how they deal with their experiences, you may not be able to tell that something dreadful has happened to them. The question is: Who foots the bill for all of this? The answer is the person who has to deal with and endure the mental, emotional, physical, and spiritual fallout that follows—the traumatized person.

The good news is that we do not have to endure it alone. What we have today that Tamar did not have in her day is the sacrificial lamb that paid it all on that rugged cross. The one whose blood was shed for the redemption of our sins that saves our souls. The one whose life and ministry shows us how our lives may stand as a testimony for others. His name is Jesus of Nazareth! So if you are still wondering how and why this book is entitled *Tamar's Healing*, that is why. In case you still do not understand why this book carries this title, continue reading. Well, I encourage you to keep reading anyhow because there still more to discover just as I have.

Part Three:

The Aftermath

Chapter Eight:

Please, Don't Go

I began this chapter as I was listening to *Life and Favor* by John P. Kee and the New Life Community Choir. The first line of this song is, "You don't know my story…." How simple yet powerfully true because there is more to me than the titles, degrees and the positions I hold. I am a mere vessel to which God is trying to use, if only I would cooperate more. What this means is I get in the way when I allow things within and outside of me to hinder and distract me. Therefore, I am not always a cooperative partner in God's divine schema for my life. I truly believe God designed me to do great things, which would effectively contribute to the up-building of God's kingdom. Yet being the human that I am I sometimes allow me to cause progress to be slowed or halted. At this point of my life, I am coming to a place where I am beginning to steer away from what the crowd says. I can hear some members of the clergy community saying, "You might want to reconsider being so transparent in this book because it don't look good." The strong willed part of me says, "I don't care how it looks! I'm called to be a vessel onto God. And if my being transparent is an issue, maybe it is not my issue." The more "politically correct" way of saying this is, "I want people to know I am human with issues just like them."

The point of this chapter is to cast down those expectations of other people and discuss some of the effects of shame which results from being violated, abused, and neglected. As indicated in one of my earlier works, "some of the very people who hold positions of prestige are the very ones whom endured a great deal of pain and shame. Their lives are a testament to the life that Jesus spoke of; in abundance. It is the story behind the glory that is important, and it is what we need to examine in this context."

In this chapter, I will discuss some of the emotional, psychological, and behavioral affects that abuse and shame may have on one's life. As you can imagine, Tamar's life following her run-in with Amnon was altered greatly. She, in effect, became a shame-based person. Based on her story, there is no real way to say Tamar was a shame-laden person because there was no real ending to her story. However, we can imagine that she was shame-based because of her choosing to live in desolation. I can only speculate on her life before being raped, but the biblical account does give us clues as to what became of Tamar's life after this episode. This will be the focus in the next few chapters—how abuse affects the lives of the shamed and abused. I must send out this disclaimer: These behaviors, thoughts, and attitudes are not limited to a person who had been raped or sexually abused. It can also be applied to other forms of abuse and neglect that also produce shame. As I go forth, you will see that a number of the characteristics go beyond those Tamar may have demonstrated. As Allender (2008) asserted in his *Wounded Heart*:

Violation of relationship opens a Pandora 's Box of suspicion and shame that exists in every person. The suspicion that we feel toward a world that has at times cavalierly ignored our longings and at other times abused our soul is like a tinder box of dry wood. Betrayal is the spark that ignites the explosive heap of mistrust in our soul. When paranoia flames, relationships is severed, hope is shattered, and belief in the other person is put on a prove-it-me basis with no opportunity for restitution. The human soul is left charred and empty, blown about by the vicious winds of loneliness and doubt (p. 120).

Where Did They Go?

I would like to think that good things will never come to an end. In my heart of hearts, I believe it when I say, "I can stay here forever." Those good moments do feel as if they will never end but many times they do. I believe we will have permanent joy in eternity. In other words, the things of this world are temporal and are intended to pass away. Just as this is true, we must also understand that life has its ups and downs that are beyond our control. There is no way around that. They are all a part of life, but there are great things awaiting us in eternity.

Unfortunately, some of us have experienced abandonment, where someone we expected to be there for us left us. This does not always include them physically leaving us because sometimes they can be right there in the same house, yet absent emotionally. However, far too many times we are left to deal with someone physically leaving us, either through death or them walking out of our lives. To the person who lives with shame, abandonment can be a devastatingly crippling issue that they wrestle with on a regular basis. Abandonment can lead to separation anxiety, where one feels discomfort when they know or imagine someone is preparing to depart for whatever reason, good or bad. Separation anxiety derives from a person who had experienced an abrupt interruption of a significant relationship, oftentimes leaving the person longing for an explanation or closure. Again, this disruption can be emotionally or physically to an individual.

Emotional abandonment could be disturbing to an individual in that it requires a person to be ignored or not supported by a person held in high regard. It is especially harmful if and when an emotional bond develops and one then cuts it off and leaves the relationship in a way that does not consider the other person's feelings/needs. Yet, when two people are in a relationship, for example, and one of them frequently feels alone. Beneath the loneliness and the pain, that person feels emotionally abandoned by the other. This can lead to shame whereby one or both people may not want to address the issues that caused the strain. The person whom was emotionally abandoned might feel it the most, particularly if they experienced this as a child, as well as the one who vacated the other's feelings. Kaufman (1992) called this "breaking the interpersonal bridge" (p. 19) and explained it in the following manner:

Breaking the interpersonal bridge is the critical event which induces shame. The experience of shame itself further severs the bridge such that an ever-widening gulf emerges between the two individuals. Their relationship has indeed become ruptured. For the young child who is so acutely aware of depending upon his parents for comfort, for his needs, for his very life, such a situation of intolerable yet unremediable isolation can generate the spectre of abandonment. What I am saying is that a young child, and a preverbal child, can directly experience shame as abandonment (p. 19).

This is how Tamar must have felt after she had time to think about what occurred in her life. I can only imagine how emotionally distraught and disappointed she was after she actually felt her father's coldness toward her, and by the fact that he did not ensure her safety and well-being. It appears that King David showed an enormous amount of indifference toward Tamar as he granted Amnon's request to send her to his home to care for him. People who are parents and are in touch with their parental instincts would have been hesitant and would have questioned Amnon's intentions; but those parents who are emotionally distant from their offspring would not pay attention to what might happen to their offspring. Kaufman (1992) described this type of non-affirming parent's behaviors toward their children as such:

> ...by becoming emotionally unavailable as, for instance, through excessively long periods of silent withdrawal from the child, this being experienced by the child as a refusal to relate; or by becoming overtly contemptuous either facially or verbally, this being experienced as complete rejection of the offense, disgusting child; or by in some manner overtly withdrawing love and prolonging this unreasonably. When the parental mood is molded by one of these reactions, whatever feelings of abandonment which may be lurking in the child can rapidly intensify to the point of sheer terror (p. 19).

What is also interesting about Tamar's relationship with her father, although the biblical account did not include this aspect, is how she reacted to being put out of Amnon's house following the rape. There were two crucial things working at the same time: Tamar felt an intense amount of shame and she felt an intense amount of unworthiness— "Tamar tore her robe and put ashes on her head" (v. 19). Using creative license for the sake of this context, let's say King David had big dreams and aspirations for Tamar, and she did not appear to possess the characteristics, the abilities, or the desire to live up to his wishes. He could have decided not to devote his time or energy to her. He could have chosen to direct his attention toward the children who showed "promise." *If Tamar were one of those children who lived up to King David's aspirations, she would have been affirmed by him and would have received his blessing as to what she could have become in her life.* Instead of blessings, it appears that Tamar was instilled with messages of shame—"If you do this, you will be that." Sorenson (2006) presented this occurrence in the following way:

> Parents also succumb to outside pressures, wanting to appear to be good parents. Without realizing it, they push their children to "look good' to the public eye, to conform to the expectations of family or community traditions while disregarding the effect on the child. In so doing, they are again actually making their own needs and feelings the priority while ignoring the child's feelings and damaging the child's self-esteem. The child feels discounted and diminished; these pictures become a part of the video he [or she] reviews throughout his [or her] life (p. 220).

As a result, the parent might utilize "emotional cut-offs" or withhold love and/or affection as a way to either get their way or pay their child back. The overall point is that when a person experiences abandonment, regardless of their age, it sets an emotional precedence whereby the person's feelings may be disturbed whenever they perceive or see behaviors in the present situation mirroring those of experiences from the past.

<u>What Did You Do?</u>

One of the most profound emotions a person experiences following a bout with abandonment is betrayal. When a person has developed trust in another person, he or she feels abandoned when the other person abruptly leaves. At the beginning of many relationships, when things are still warm and fuzzy, people tend to feel and express wishes for things to stay the same: "Promise me you'll never leave me." In order to keep things going, the other person will pledge: "I will never leave you." Their intentions may be good because, while the relationship is in its infancy, they really cannot say they will be in it for the long haul. If things get rough, some people will try to tough it out. They will hang in there and try to work it out or they will leave. These solutions can and will lead to acts of betrayal where one or both people will feel the intense residual effects of infidelity caused by the other.

Depending on the people involved in the relationship, closure might be achieved amicably. However, for the person who was socialized in a chaotic environment or they experienced or witnessed volatile break-ups, peaceful separations may not be something they can accomplish or live with. This is especially true for the person who experienced being abandoned and/or betrayed. Dayton (1997) wrote the following about intimate relationships and people who grew up where emotional shut offs were utilized frequently:

> Experiencing powerful feelings in intimate love relationships can feel frightening to a person who has learned to shut feelings down in earlier intimate relationships. We learn how to be intimate very early in life and we carry that learning with us into partnership and family (p. 77).

At this point, I cannot say this was the case for Tamar. However, I can say she could have felt an enormous amount of betrayal because the people she felt should have protected her did not. I can also say Tamar felt betrayed by those she trusted not to exploit and hurt her. Therefore, Tamar's ability to cope with being left unprotected and to recover from what happened to her was inextricably diminished. In effect, she learned that she was not worthy of being protected and her view on future relationships was bleak. "When the lessons learned on how to be intimate are not conducive to creating intimacy," Dayton said, "it is difficult to sustain such relationships later on in life" (1997, p. 90).

It is an unfortunate reality that we will experience situations and relationships that will leave hurtful impressions on our psyches, but they can be useful to us as we continue to live with and relate to others. Yet if these experiences and feelings are not addressed or processed appropriately, a pattern of unsuccessful relationships can continue throughout a person's life. Dayton (1997) further explained:

> When, as adults, we enter intimate relationships without a willingness to resolve old grief, recognize the effects of early childhood traumas, work through those traumas and learn relationship skills, we run the risk of setting ourselves up for failure and acting out pain in our current relationship... When two adults try to be intimate, the children they once were are called to the stage of the relationship; mysteriously they come forward along with the feeling, thinking, and behavior that they experienced as children. The grown man who as a little boy learned not to share his vulnerable feelings will find it very hard to do that in an intimate adult relationship. The grown woman who learned to please others and deny her own desires will likely continue that pattern in her adult relationships (p. 90).

Therefore, persons whom have developed such patterns may be the ones who will blame the other person for leaving the relationship and betraying them. Unless this person puts forth an effort to examine himself or herself and heal from previous hurtful relationships, they are prone to repeat some of the same behaviors and/or attitudes developed during and as a result of other relationships. In effect, he or she might use mechanisms they believe will help protect them from feeling let down in their current and future relationships. One of those mechanisms people use when they have not addressed or healed from failed relationships is emotional numbness. Dayton (1997) made the following observations:

Emotional numbness inhibits a person's ability to respond to the subtle vicissitudes of any relationship. It is a defense against strong feelings, and because intimate relationships contain powerful emotions, the inability to feel or stay with them works against the partner's ability to remain present in an emotionally charged relationship climate. It works on subtler levels as well, decreasing a person's willingness to move in and out of aspects of the relationship that require staying present with strong feelings. In order to communicate feelings, it is necessary first to feel and describe them within the self and then find words to communicate that inner world to the other person. The partner of someone who is emotionally numb can feel frustrated, as if he or she has lost access to or is disconnected from the emotional world of the other person (pp. 80 -81).

Although people in intimate relationships actively attempt to achieve intimacy, the existence of unresolved issues lived and learned in their lives can prevent them from doing so. Not addressing feelings of being abandoned and/or being betrayed will continue to have residual effects on intimate relationships one may venture into.

I Don't See It That Way

When I read into the portion of Tamar's story presented at the beginning of this chapter, I found a number of dynamics at work and many were not in Tamar's favor. In the exchange where Absalom attempted to comfort Tamar in verse twenty, it appears that he wanted her to stop hurting, while keeping her mouth closed about who was the cause of her pain. Let's look at verse twenty again: "Her brother Absalom saw her and asked, 'Is it true that Amnon has been with you? Well, my sister, keep quiet for now, since he's your brother. Don't you worry about it.' So Tamar lived as a desolate woman in her brother Absalom's house." Being that Absalom was her brother; Tamar probably went to him because she trusted him and believed he would help her. From this exchange, Tamar surely could have developed a deep sense of distrust. Tamar could have gone to Absalom seeking comfort, but what she got instead a gag order to not say anything to anyone because Amnon was their brother. How demoralizing it must have been for Tamar.

For Tamar, and people like her, trust is something that is not easily given or achieved. Oftentimes aguish and pain renders a scorned heart incapable of allowing that person to trust someone else with their feelings. This makes achieving the openness that accompanies trust that is needed to have an intimate relationship very difficult. Trusting another person to care for one's heart and feelings are called upon to permit one to bare their soul before another person. Bradshaw (2005) explained it in the following terms:

> Intimacy requires the ability to be vulnerable. To be intimate is to risk exposing our inner selves to each other, to bare our deepest feelings, desires and thoughts. To be intimate is to be the very ones we are and to love and accept each other unconditionally. This requires self-confidence and courage. Such courage creates a new space in our relationship. That space is not yours or mine; it is ours (p. 235).

92

Betrayal in any relationship is a form of one breaking promises made to the other. It is akin to outwardly lying to the other person without any intentions of fulfilling the agreement they made with the other person. Trusting is not an easy feat for the one who has unresolved disappointments and brushes with disloyal acts committed against them. Holcomb and Holcomb (2001) described betrayal in terms of sin when they wrote: "...it is a sin betraying trust and destroying relationships between victims and those who should have cared for them but instead caused them harm. The consequences of this sin is that it creates barriers of trust for victims in their future relationships" (p. 169). Thus, causing one to become distrusting of others and also sparking behaviors that are indicative of suspicion such as paranoia, and believing people are plotting or conspiring against them.

How sad for Tamar to have had to lived as an emotionally deserted woman in Absolam's house? Many of us, myself included, live a life that is devoid of intimacy in romantic relationships as well as other types of relationships. This demonstrates varying levels of distrust and the lowering of one's self-esteem. Sorenson (2006) accounted for this when she wrote:

> Past hurtful situations have confused those with LSE (low self-esteem); now they do not know whom or when to trust. Some become skeptical and distrustful of everyone; others in their neediness and loneliness have difficulty discerning when they can trust someone and when they should not, often making poor choices. Believing they are unworthy, children grow into adults who have difficulty trusting those

who say they care, those who make commitments... Being treated as "less than" convinces these people that they are "damaged," that they will always be inferior. When friends and loved ones try to convince them differently, they wonder' they feel patronized. The best of intentions, the most sincere compliments then fall on deaf ears (p. 212).

This quotation felt as though the writer was speaking directly to me! Out of desperation, I met, dated and proposed marriage to my second fiancé. Initially, I was skeptical of her intentions because I did not feel I was worthy of her company; let alone her attention, love and commitment. Each time she or my friends tried to convince me that she was honored to be with me as well, these words of encouragement only reinforced my feelings of not being worthy of having an intimate relationship that was true and transparent. For such a long time, I could not put my finger on the source of this point of view until I read: "The idea that one may be at the core, unlovable, is devastating to consider" (Sorenson, 2006, p. 208). Eventually, my behaviors escalated to complete distrust of her; and then, ultimately self-sabotage. Again, those whom have lived through abandonment and betrayal are now distrusting of others; and it becomes very difficult for them to trust again. In *Shame: The Power of Caring*, Kaufman (1992) wrote:

Letting another person become significant to us means that person's caring, respect or valuing have begun to matter. We permit ourselves the vulnerability associated with needing something from that other person. We look to that person for something. And we expect some response to our needs, whether expressed clearly or not. Experiencing a need and expecting a response can be viewed as two sides of one and the same phenomenological event... The interpersonal bridge is built upon certain expectations which we have come to accept and to depend upon. Learning to expect a certain mutuality of response is the basis for the trust we feel for someone significant to us. Shame is likely whenever our most basic expectations of a significant other are suddenly exposed as wrong. To have someone valued unexpectedly betray our trust opens the self inside of us and exposes it to view (p. 14).

I Don't Believe My Own Eyes

In the previous section, one of the passages I included from Sorenson (2006, p. 212), who made reference to people with hurtful pasts developing patterns where they make "poor choices" and accept unfavorable treatment from others because they feel "inferior" or undeserving of love. In effect, they are "damaged goods." This mentality comes from unsuccessful and abusive relationships, which are reflective of people with poor, injured concepts of themselves. After experiencing these types of relationships for some time, the person's inferior perception of themselves are strengthened by repeatedly engaging in similar relationships. Unfortunately, the person's vision is skewed, and his or her ability to discern healthy relationships that may be beneficial is grossly impaired. In other words, he or she cannot see a good thing when it comes, as if to say, "I don't believe my own eyes."

This type of thinking and/or attitude is not only typical of people with low self-esteem but also of people whom had to endure being abused in the past. By the way, many people who had been abused are the very ones who live with low self-esteem. So what happens when someone comes along and tries to love that person for who they really are? He or she will shut the other person out, engage in self-sabotaging behaviors, or abruptly end the relationship when it becomes too intense. All of these behaviors are indicative of a person that is afraid of intimacy or being in committed relationships, with good reason.

Being vulnerable or baring one's self before another person *is* called intimacy. Before I go further, let's look at what constitutes intimacy. According to *Merriam-Webster's Dictionary and Thesaurus* (2007), intimacy is defined as "the state of being intimate; something of the personal or private nature." The synonyms for intimacy are "closeness, familiarity, nearness" (p. 436). I wanted to include these delineations in order to say intimate relationships are not limited to romantic relationships. Intimate relationships are those relationships where people achieve closeness by connecting to one another. Think of an intimate relationship as you would an electrical circuit. If that circuit is connected and the energy is allowed to flow from one end to the other, then that circuit will operate as it should. Yet, if that circuit is disconnected or if there is a short somewhere along the way, then the circuit will not allow the energy to flow freely; thereby leaving the circuit broken, in effect, inefficient. Both scenarios are seen in intimate relationships. To take the former situation further, if too much energy is being pushed through this faulty circuit, an overload can and will occur. This overload is what we call a black out or a blown fuse.

People who fear intimacy can be compared to the

circuit that is broken or failing to make the proper connection. The connection, in this regard, is one person not allowing energy to be exerted or received by the other person. In order to establish and maintain a relationship of any kind, trust is a vital key—meaning, both parties must trust one another. It is quite difficult for a person who has a fear of intimacy because it is likely that they do not trust others. So when a person does find him- or herself in a situation where intense feelings are present, it might be a frightening experience for him or her. Therefore, he or she feels forced to run away, both emotionally and physically, from the other person.

* * * * *

I had to take a break from writing to examine myself. I engaged in an exercise I learned while I was in therapy some years ago—it's called introspective reflection. This exercise calls for one to channel thought-filled energy on a particular subject. I chose to focus on my relational life before the incident. For the life of me, I could not recall having many problems with intimacy. I had several romantic relationships, many friends, and was willing and able to maintain several close friendships, some of which I am still involved in to this very day. But something happened to me after being violated. I became distant and somewhat guarded with people had I met since then and some I met before then. To be more precise, I would only allow people to get close to a certain extent. I read the following: "Shame-filled people long for intimacy but are deeply afraid their defectiveness will be exposed. Thus, they tend to sabotage relationships as they begin to get intimate" (Tracy 2005, p. 82). Not only did these

97

words ring true, but they also helped me understand I am a shame-filled person. It explained why I am reluctant, in so many ways, when it comes to other people and intimacy.

I also came to understand something that was quite interesting after writing and reading the preceding paragraph: I do have some characteristics of a shame-filled person, and many of my relational, self-sabotaging behaviors have decreased, sometimes some of those behaviors do try to creep back into my present life. For example, I used cut people out of my life when I felt that they betrayed me, were getting too close, or if I felt overwhelmed by their presence, which did not necessarily mean he or she did something hurtful to me. Keep in mind I have already established that intimacy is not limited to romantic relationships only. Intimacy is the closeness, the relating to and the sharing between people. In a recent incident, I found myself torn between my old behavioral patterns and my new way of relating, rising within me. A person I had the opportunity to spend a lot of time with was almost cut off because I was starting to really relate to them to the point where I could feel this person's moods, thoughts and feelings. However, this person withheld vital information and denied various questions to which I knew the answers to for quite some time. I began ruminating over the possibility that this person could not be trusted. I vacillated between confronting them and just letting them go. Finally, my emotional mind said, "Cut them off while the getting is good." After thinking about it and weighing the two options once more, I prayed about it and waited. I decided to wait until the time was right and the person appeared to be ready for this type of conversation.

When it came time for me to make a move, I still did not know what I was going to do about the situation. I have to admit that I had to stifle thoughts that were shouting: "Cut this off now!" Instead of speaking or doing anything, I stilled those thoughts and waited for the "still, small voice" that eventually asked the question, "What do you feel?" Baffled by this question, I asked myself the same question in my silence. What I felt was fear. The other person was afraid to say what was on their mind out of fear that "I would disappoint you. You would get mad at me." That was their rationale but what I felt was frustration and impatience with the other person. I realized my irritation and intolerance derived from me wanting the other person to "hurry up and let me in." Developing relationships that are intimate in nature do not happen easily or quickly for anyone. Kaufman and Raphael (1991) offered an explanation to clarify the establishing and the growth of intimate relationships when they wrote:

> Real relationships take building and nurturing slowly over time before a sense of certainty about that relationship takes root. Intimacy and caring evolve within a real and secure relationship. It may take anywhere from six months to a year for a relationship to become solid and certain for both participants. Real caring does not flourish easily or quickly, but must be actively worked for by both individuals in a relationship... ...it is useful to be extremely wary of "instant intimacy" or attempts at rushing a relationship. Good relationships take slow and careful building over many months. It is necessary to observe the other person consciously in a variety of situations over time in order to know just what kind

of individual he or she is. It also takes time and repeated contact to develop ease and comfort with one another. And it takes time to build the day-by-day supports which make any relationship work. Six months to a year is a more realistic expectation regarding the length of time needed to feel a sense of certainty about a new relationship. Intimacy or caring are not instant, but grow naturally in their own time. It is wiser not to attempt to rush them because relationships which become too close too quickly often blow apart. Sound relationships evolve gradually and require conscious attention. Living consciously in the world is the best safeguard (pp. 9 - 10, 104).

This passage contains key signs of growth for me, and helped me to feel confident in my wavering, that I was growing in terms of learning to relate to others by allowing them to relate to me. Without really reading or studying materials, as I began to work through my trust issues, and give people a chance to know me; I discovered I had already began to use some of the principles that Kaufman and Raphael (1991) presented in their work. In addition, after reading this passage, the writers further inspired me to utilize them over and over again, "Then our ability to care will flourish more soundly" (p. 104).

Chapter Nine:

I'm Gonna Hide

"To all my enemies I have become a reproach, but especially to my neighbors, and a dread to my acquaintances, who flee from me on the street. I am forgotten like a dead man, and out of mind; like a broken vessel am I. For I have heard the slander of many; terror is on every side! While they schemed together against me, they plotted to take my life. But I trusted in, relied on, and was confident in You, O Lord; I said, You are my God. My times are in Your hands; deliver me from the hands of my foes and those who pursue me and persecute me. Let Your face shine on Your servant; save me for Your mercy's sake and in Your loving-kindness. Let me not be put to shame, O Lord, or disappointed, for I am calling upon You; let the wicked be put to shame, let them be silent in Sheol (the place of the dead). Let the lying lips be silenced which speak insolently against the [consistently] righteous with pride and contempt. Oh, how great is Your goodness, which You have laid up for those who frat, revere, and worship You, goodness which You have wrought for those who trust and take refuge in You before the sons of men! In the secret place of Your presence You hide them from the plots of me; You keep them secretly in Your pavilion from the strife of tongues (Psalm 31: 11 – 20, *AMB*).

Tormented from the Inside

What is more lethal than living with poison inside your body? I believe living with harmful, infectious emotional baggage that continually causes you pain to fester in your system is just as lethal. What I mean by this is, living, functioning, and believing the negative information you have acquired in your life that does not motivate, encourage, or inspire you to reach your greatest potential. In the last chapter, I mentioned the fact that our lives are shaped and bound by how we are socialized—this is not only limited by our childhood experiences. The human condition is predicated on our ability to receive constant affirmation and inspiration, whether it is life giving or life draining. In his work, entitled, *The Psychology of Shame*, Kaufman (1996) wrote the following passage that emphasizes the need and the affects of receiving continuous affirmation from significant others:

> The need for affirmation is the need for valuing, recognition, and admiration. Children need to feel singled out and openly valued. To feel recognized as a unique self is central to self development... When a child is admired, that child feels affirmed. To be admired by another is to be gazed upon with deepening enjoyment, to be openly smiled upon. It is the gleam in the parent's eyes along with the smile on the parent's face. Admiration from a parent also mirrors back to the self the self's own joy. Affirmation of self is a recurring need, observed in adulthood no less than in childhood. It is not a sign of deficit, but an expression of a fundamental need central to human maturation and to the optimal functioning of the self. ...Throughout life, individuals experience moments of self-doubt.

Effectively navigating such crisis is vital because each individual needs to continue feeling that the person within, the inner self, is still worthwhile and valued. Through having someone significant directly provide that affirmation of self one is enabled to give it to oneself. A self-affirming capacity thereby emerges. ***Through developing this inner source of valuing, individuals cease being entirely dependent on the evaluations of others for their own of self-worth and esteem*** (p. 77, emphasis mine).

Affirmation is an important part of our lives because it has restorative factors which are vital to our ability to sustain mental and emotional stability, as well as physical health. In this section, I will discuss ways in which suffering revisits the individual when he or she chooses not to work through difficult emotional shame experienced in their lives. I will include the affects of how the social environment also impedes emotional rejuvenation and growth.

I had a talk with a close friend regarding someone they knew. This person had been "happily" married since the mid-1990s to a person, by all external appearances, she loved and adored. My friend expressed some concerns because she knew this couple, particularly the husband, beyond the social realm. My friend stated the husband made some remarks that really caused her to stop and ponder on the deeper meaning of his statements. After giving some thought to this, my friend invited the husband to lunch to discuss the comments made and how she felt about what was said. My friend and this couple come from a tradition where the church is the center of their lives and the teachings therein significantly weighed in their lives. The couple in question believes that their marriage *had* to last until death separated them. This concept is not uncommon and it is an awesome concept to aspire to in their lives together, however....

My friend and the husband decided on a late lunch in order avoid having to rush and return to work or home. My friend wanted to approach this discussion in a way that was non-combative or aggressive because, after all, the subject matter was very sensitive in nature. What was concerning to my friend was it appeared that the husband indirectly voiced feelings of not being very happy as he once was in his marriage. In one of his statements he indicated he felt belittled at times and that he was not able to freely express his thoughts and feelings for fear of being ostracized by his wife and other family members. He also mentioned that when he feels "misunderstood by some things I don't know I'm doing, it is misread by others." Therefore, most alarmingly, he places more effort and energy towards "making sure my facial expressions and body language is inviting and friendly." The husband was a serious person for the most part because of his occupation and his personality. So naturally, his outward expressions were misconstrued by others, even by those he believes should know him best.

My friend shared that she allowed the husband to open this portion of their conversation and waited for him to invite her input, without diving her straight into her concerns. The husband explained how much he valued her friendship and that her opinion was important to him because she had proven to be "a good friend" to him. The husband continued on to say he had been struggling with these feelings, his family-of-origin's ethos, and the church's teachings for several years. He emphasized that there were times when these feelings were surpassed by many good times because his family loved him and he loved them, "but I think we may not be traveling in the same direction anymore." This statement brought tears to his eyes. My friend encouraged him to express his feelings and how they might be affecting him. The husband replied, "I feel ashamed to be thinking and feeling this way because I was taught marriage is forever, 'til death do us part. Each time I think about talking to my wife about what I feel I end up talking myself out of it because of how I might be perceived." My friend shared her support of the husband with her presence but felt conflicted by what was said by the husband. My friend said she wanted consultation on dealing with the shame attached to the husband's situation and the feelings that accompanied it. My immediate response was that the shame was derived from the husband's indoctrination and how it was maintained by those around him, even if they did not intend to cause him harm or pain.

If you recall, one of the aspects of shame is that it is described as a "very heavy feeling" (Smedes, 1993, p. 5). For this husband, his feeling ashamed originated from his upbringing and his current social environment, which encompassed his family and church teachings and religious life. Unfortunately, it does not seem that this man was encouraged to pursue his God-given will to live and seek aspirations for himself without feeling overwhelmingly ashamed. Malone (2006) spoke to this as he wrote from his personal experience from his own family and being a pastor:

In the family, we are accepted, approved and loved—

or we are rejected, disowned and treated with indifference. If any of the latter occurs in our life, we learn shame at an early age. Young children are not aware of what is happening to them and do not have the skills to protect themselves. So it's open season on children for shame to develop in them... Families shame children when they do not own them. I am not talking about slavery or ownership in that sense, but rather about the acceptance of a child and the verbal acknowledgement that, "This child is mine, he belongs, and he is my future...." (p. 61).

You may also recall the concept of ownership that was discussed earlier. But yet it came up again some chapters later. Shame induces separation, not belonging to others. However, Malone (2006) continued on to address how the church affects the person's inner-self when he wrote:

Going to church should be an uplifting experience. However, in many cases, you come away feeling depressed and shamed. Many churches place their greatest emphasis on how we have failed to please God. Christianity has become a performance rather than a relationship for many. You must try harder, do more, and be more dedicated than ever before... Unfortunately, early in my 45-year ministry, I fell into this trap. On Sunday as people left the service, they would often say, "Pastor, you sure did step on my toes today." Foolishly, I thought that meant I had succeeded because I had made them feel guilty. Such doctrines and teachings cause the negative to stand tall and strong—we are forced to focus on our failures, rather than on encouragement from a God who has forgiven all our sins and loves us with His whole heart. God is not trying to hurt us, He is trying to heal us and make us whole. ...Sadly we have often made the church a major place of shame for the believer. But, if I understand Scripture correctly, when God forgives my sins, he puts them away from me "as far as the east is from the west." I am glad He did not say "as far as the north is from the south...." (pp. 69 – 70).

What this author is saying, in my estimation, is that we are allowing the church to become a source of consternation in that the proclamation of salvation and liberty is not being espoused to its members. Instead, more and more people are being wrapped up in the bondage of guilt and shame because the messages tend to be brow-beating rather than the conviction of sin, without the repentance of sin; therefore, further inducing shame upon its members, and in so doing pushing them further into their shame-filled experiences.

Some of this is derived from our early socialization within our families-of-origin. I once heard one of the elders say (and I paraphrase): "It behooves us not to consider our past because we go aimlessly into the night of life." Wilson (1990), in her discussion of the childhood within the family, admonishes us in our adult life in the following way:

Understanding your childhood family environment and how it influences you today will mean seeing it through adult eyes. You might remember many of the basic facts about your childhood, but you might see them only through the eyes of a frightened child. In effect, you are living your life based on choices you made as a confused, and perhaps abused, child with a distorted view of reality. You need wisdom and insight to gain a truthful perspective on your past and present and to have an accurate context for changing your future (p. 36).

This might have been where the husband was functioning out of in his adult life. His experiences within his family-of-origin vastly influenced his views on his adult life. It appears that he was living to prove that he was living up to some unspoken standards placed on him by his family-of-origin while suppressing his need to be affirmed and express himself freely. He found himself doing so outside of his immediate and church families in that he talked with my friend. Although he did not say this, I believe he did so because he learned to find a trustworthy individual to serve as an outlet, one who would allow him to be himself without fear of being judged and/or shamed for doing so. Kaufman (1992), in his discussion of "Defending Strategies Against Shame," taught: "…variables influencing the selection of defense concerns the particular patterns of affect, drive, and need socialization with a given family" (p. 79). In other words, the husband chose a way to protects himself from present or impending harm based on his family's life and environment. Kaufman further elucidated on this concept in the following powerful expression:

The way in which the expression of affects, drives, and needs is handled in a specific family also makes available ready means of defense. Likewise, the dynamics of the particular family as a social group counts heavily in the selective sorting out of whatever useful means of adaptation may be at hand... Adaption is what defenses are all about. Defenses are learned because they are the best means available to the child for survival. Defending strategies are adaptive and have survival value. *That is the natural reason they come about.* If they were not necessary or did not work at all, we would be most unlikely to develop them. ...Depending upon the nature of the supporting human environment in which the child matures, defenses can either remain flexible and positive or else can become rigidly relied upon and, hence, internalized as armaments for the self (pp. 79 – 80, emphasis mine).

Our ability to adapt and protect ourselves is contingent upon our ability to assess and adjust those defense strategies learned from childhood, and our willingness or ability to adjust and utilize methods that alleviates pain—both presently and in the future.

I'll Just Hide

When a person fails to develop and/or use healthy methods to protect and defend him- or herself from immediate or imminent harm, the likelihood of he or she utilizing other means to cope, such as drugs, alcohol, gambling, pornography, promiscuity, and many other self-destructive behaviors are more probable. In this segment, I will address at least two less obvious methods (or defense mechanisms) that many people use to protect themselves or to escape from conditions that present a threat to his or her physical or emotional being. To the untrained eye, one may not recognize or understand what these actions are or what they might mean. Numbing and dissociation (or splitting) will be discussed. It is befitting that I give more attention to these behaviors because if utilized improperly, these coping mechanisms can present dangerous situations and further complicate things for the individual.

At one point in my life, I began to notice that quite a few people voluntarily started sharing their stories of being sexually abused or violated with me. I thought it was strange because the timing of these disclosures came when I was in the process of searching for my niche in life after earning my doctorate. I can recall two people saying something like "Can I tell you something I haven't talked about to many people" in one week. One person came to me to talk about one of her "close friends." As this person went into detail about some of the incidents their friend had endured, I thought it was odd that she knew so many intricate details about her friend's situation. Then, again, I did not think about it too hard because I figured this close friend could have told their story to this person several times. I had to really put forth extra effort in listening to this person, who really seemed concerned about her friend. A part of my mental energy went toward praying for direction, because, as I said early, this was one of a few people to disclose sexual abuse within a few days, even though this discussion was about a "friend." As this person continued to talk to me, I noticed that her demeanor drastically changed as her voice did not. I sat still for a moment and she noticed my body language and asked, "What's wrong? Is this too much?" Without missing a beat,

I asked, "Why are you telling me all of this? How do you know I can be trusted with this information?" She was stunned by these two simple questions. She said, "Well, I don't know why all of this is coming out right now, but your spirit makes it easy for me to talk. The person I'm talking about is me. I was the one sexually abused several times in my life." I noticed that she found solace in speaking of herself in the third party and this could have been her way of protecting herself, but I did not over-analyze it because making assumptions about people is not a good thing. However, soon after this disclosure she drifted off into a daydream-like state as she continued to tell her story. It was kind of troublesome for me because I used this tactic in my life and I felt that she had not dealt with these incidents in a healthy way; therefore, she may have been struggling with these issues at that time. But as for me, I had learned not to use this defense mechanism unless it was absolutely necessary. Well, she came out of her gaze moments later and engaged in a lively conversation about children. This person learned how to numb her feelings, even when she talked about those painful experiences from a third-person perspective.

Another instance that led me to the direction for this section and my vocation was when I began working with a teenage girl, who was referred to me by her mother. Out of frustration, the mother said her child was distant and behaved strangely. "I think something's wrong with her," she divulged. I decided that I would establish a relationship with this teen and not subject her to further complications because she knew I counseled troubled teenagers. After observing her for a couple of weeks, engaging in small talk, and simply checking in with her from time to time, somehow I got this teen to sit down and talk with me for a few moments. By the time we prepared to part, the teen asked, "Can I talk to you about something when I'm ready?" I agreed and gave her one of my business cards. I instructed her to text me when she was ready to talk to which she agreed. Weeks passed without a text or any other means of communication from this teen, but I knew not to question her about not making the first move. I wanted her to feel comfortable enough to initiate this conversation.

One night, while at work, my cell phone lit up and vibrated for a few seconds, which was indicative of several text messages coming in one behind the other. It turned out to be a long message from the teenage girl, who wanted to talk to me and wanted to give me a "heads-up" about what she wanted to talk about. I acknowledged my receipt of her message and asked if I could meet with her face-to-face because I was at work and did not want to do so over the phone. She agreed and we chose a day I would come to her home when her mother was present. On the day of this appointment, I went about my day as usual but felt something strange in the air. I set out to travel to the teen's home and pulled into her driveway when my cell phone rang. It was the teen's mother, who sounded a bit panicked. She asked, "Can you come over to see what going on? She's acting weird and she's just sitting still with this strange look on her face." I informed her that I was walking up the stairs of her front porch. The teen's mother rushed to the door to let me in and said while pointing, "She's over here." The mother led me to the kitchen area where the teen quietly sat with tears streaming down her cheeks. I slid into a chair near the teen trying not to disturb her. Her mother impatiently demanded, "Well! What's wrong with her?" I remained silent as I began to pray. Soon the teen wiped her tears and asked, "Mom, can you please give us some privacy?" The mother was shocked because apparently the teen had not spoken one word in the past couple of hours. I grabbed and squeezed the mother's hand gently to reassure her that it would be fine. I also asked the teen if I could explain confidentiality to her mother to which she agreed with a big sigh.

After I spoke with the teenager's mother for a few moments, I returned to the kitchen area and found the teen composed and relaxed. I took my seat without speaking for a few moments. The teen started speaking without prompting from me. She apologized profusely "for zoning out like that and scaring my mother." The teen indicated that this was "the first time I did that since that day...," she said without completing her statement. She hung her head and discontinued eye contact with me for a few moments. I gave her additional latitude because whatever took place "that day" was traumatic for her. After a few moments of silence the teen went on to say:

> There was this boy I liked a lot and I thought he liked me too. We started talking a lot, and I wanted us to become more than friends, as in boyfriend and girlfriend. I really liked him but I was not interested in having a sexual relationship at that time, and we talked about this, too. One day he asked me if I wanted to go over one of our mutual friends' house because he had a new girlfriend and thought it would cool for us to hang out with them. I told my boyfriend I didn't mind going and asked my mom if I could go. We walked to his friend's house after school one day and had a good time talking, laughing and joking around with each other. He was in a good mood, and I thought it was because he was spending time with me. Well, we arrived at the house and our

friend said his girlfriend was on her way and that her mother would be dropping her off. The three of us laughed and joked for a while, and then, the boys' faces became serious. My friend looked at me and said, "So won't you let him do you." I was shocked and scared because I had never had sex before and I did not plan to that day.

The teen began to slip back into her fixed gaze as she continued to mutter some words. I immediately encouraged her to stay in the room with me. I asked her if she could recall her state-of-mind on the day in question. She became animated and said, "Yes, it was like I left the room while they did whatever they did to me." The teen softly said, "I know they did something to me because, because I'm not a virgin anymore." I shifted the focus a bit to ask the teen if this was the first time she had "left the room." She replied, "I used to do it to ignore people, but never that long." The teen explained some details that indicated she was in a dissociative state for at least an hour or so. I recognized what was occurring immediately and asked the teen if she wanted to talk to me once a week to which she agreed and said, "There is so much more to get off my chest."

* * * * *

In these two short stories, both individuals used numbing and dissociative behaviors to ease their pain from the events in which they were mistreated. Dissociation (or splitting) and numbing are two misunderstood behaviors because they can appear to be daydreaming, spacing out, or

114

not paying attention to what is going on; while, the latter can be misconstrued as one being distant and/or "playing games."

I want take some time to address these concepts more because they are more prevalent than many people realize. I am very familiar with them because they are also a part of my own defense system. Dissociating and numbing can appear to be the same behavior at times; however, they differ in many ways. So let's start with dissociation. When people dissociate, they pull away from what is happening to or around themselves. A person uses this mechanism to protect themselves emotionally and mentally. Many would go into what can be described as a trance or a dreamlike state. The *Diagnostic and Statistical Manual of Mental Disorders* (*DSM-5*, 2013) describes a dissociative trance in the following manner:

> This condition is characterized by an acute narrowing or complete loss of awareness of immediate surroundings that manifest as profound unresponsiveness or insensitivity to environmental stimuli. The unresponsiveness may be accompanied by minor stereotyped behaviors (e. g., finger movements) of which the individual is unaware and/or that he or she cannot control, as well as transient paralysis or loss of consciousness. The dissociative trance is not a normal part of a broadly accepted collective cultural or religious practice (pp. 158 – 159).

What brings these episodes about is what the *DSM-5* also explained as "Acute dissociative reactions to stressful events" in the ensuing fashion:

> ...transient condition that typically last less than 1 month, and sometimes only a few hours or days. These conditions are characterized by constriction of consciousness; depersonalization; derealization; perceptual disturbances (e. g., time slowing, macropsia); micro-amnesias; transient stupor; and/or alterations in sensory-motor functioning (e. g. analgesia, paralysis) (p. 158).

In terms of defense mechanisms, Maltz (2012), in her discussion of automatic reactions, wrote the following:

> Automatic reactions are activated, or triggered, by something in our present-day reality that reminds us, either consciously or unconsciously, of the past abuse. The trigger can be almost anything: an object, a picture, a touch, a movement, a smell, a sound, a setting, a sensation, a physical characteristic, or a feeling such as fear, abandonment, or anxiety...
> ...many of our automatic reactions were learned as a way to cope with the mental and physical stress experienced in the abuse. Victims may begin dissociating for instance, to sidestep anything from pain to pleasure. Dissociating also allows victims to cooperate with the offender and thus avoid further violence and pain. This reaction can enable a victim to retain a sense of power and self. ...For many survivors, especially those who were victimized repeatedly, the process of *dissociating* becomes

something they do over and over again... (pp. 146 -
147).

Collins (2001) also stated:

The actual mechanism of dissociation is considered
by many to be autohypnotic. That is, autohypnosis is
used defensively to protect or remove the individual
from unpleasant situations that the individual has no
control over. The use of autohypnosis, as a
successful method for passing through a difficult
situation, is then generalized as a coping strategy for
other lesser stresses (p. 1).

The reason why I asked the teenage girl if she started
"leaving the room" or ignoring people in that manner was my
way of getting an idea or some sign of this child's life in terms
of abuse. As it turned out, she started dissociating to stave
off what she perceived as emotional and verbal abuse from
her mother. This became "a way of thinking that put
emotional distance between themselves and the abuse, and
memories of the abuse" Stone (2004, p. 27) explained. To a
certain extent, dissociating helps a person to step away from
the situation for the moment in order to separate themselves,
mentally and emotionally, from being sucked into it. But the
writer continued on to state the following:

For example, many survivors talk of 'leaving' their
bodies, viewing the experience of abuse as if watching
from a corner of the room. Or some simply "forget"
the experience altogether. Dissociation made it easier

to separate feelings from behaviors, but as experts know today, in spite of our mental efforts to make them go away, such traumas can still surface as sleepless, flashbacks, and fears of impeding dooms (Stone, 2004, p. 27).

In a sense, dissociating does give the person relief in that the person does not have to face their perpetrator or abuser in that moment. In other words, "Dissociation does not take the abuse away, it takes the person away" (Tracy, 2005, p. 100).

Numbing, like dissociating, is a defense mechanism that helps the person disconnect from an abusive situation. Numbing is the lingering effect of the abusive incident(s). Tracy (2005) addressed numbing in the following statement:

Numbing (also called "constriction") is the emotional condition that results from overwhelming trauma. Internally, it involves the shutting down of all feelings so that, instead of feeling pain, one simply feels nothing. Externally, it has been described as a "reduced responsiveness to the outside world." Sometimes abuse survivors are aware of shutting down emotionally, but in cases of extreme, particularly chronic trauma… Numbing can also take place long after the original trauma, when abuse survivors shut down all feelings (pleasurable and painful). No feelings seem preferable to painful and confusing feelings (p. 100).

Both numbing and dissociating do have protective

qualities, however, they can be disruptive if the traumatic experience is not processed in a way that helps the person make appropriate adjustments in his or her life. Tracy (2005) further explained in the ensuing passage:

> Since one of the primary trauma effects is numbing (or constriction)—shutting down emotionally—it's easy to see how abuse survivors often experience little or no relational intimacy. Numbing means that abuse victims don't feel anything, be it pain or pleasure. They don't feel their own feelings, nor can they recognize and embrace the feelings of others… In shutting down to avoid pain, abuse survivors also miss out on love (pp. 114 – 115).

Another aspect of utilizing numbing and/or dissociating repeatedly as a primary defense mechanism is that the duration that he or she remains in this state can increase and this may be detrimental to one's overall well being. This was the case of the teenage girl mentioned above. My immediate concern for her not only dealt with her emotional and mental self, but also her physical self. In detailing what she observed once she "came back in the room" mentally—her story is too graphic for this context—I wanted her to understand the need for her to be examined by a physician as soon as possible. Because of her age, I also knew there were some things to be processed in order to help her deal with, work through, and come to some understanding about relationships and intimacy. This courageous young woman-child told her mother about the incident with me there for support, and declared, "I will not let them get the best of me. I'm a child of God." She

119

hugged her mother for a few moments as they cried together and she asked to be taken to the emergency room to be checked for pregnancy and sexually transmitted/venereal diseases. The next time I saw her, she announced, "All came back negative. Now let's get to work!" Her mother smiled and shed tears of joy as she reported her child was presenting as "focused and determined." This young woman-child inspired me to really consider how I processed my own situation and relational dealings with others. I praise God for the deliverance this wonderful young woman experienced. The bit of news I heard about her was that she was finishing up her work and was preparing to graduate with her Master's degree in Clinical Child Psychology and she was engaged to be married.

I would be remiss if I did not discuss the dark side of when numbing and dissociation are combined. To be honest, I tried to stay away from it because I knew I would be required to go to through some painful places in the traces of my mind—some memories I would rather disappear but they are a part of my story. I knew far in advance that these images would creep up during this writing process, so I solicited the supportive help of my good friend, Glennisha, to be on standby in case I went too far into these memories. During my reading and research, I came across the passage listed below. It reminded me of two times in my life when I used other things and other people to get away from what I was experiencing in mind. While reading Woodley's (2013) book entitled, *A Wildflower Grows in Brooklyn*, I came across the following brutally honest passage:

Since I couldn't escape the pain in my home or in my heart I quickly learned to numb it. The drug of choice during my teenage years was pot. I smoked a lot of it with my boyfriend Brian. I didn't really like the feeling after I smoked it but I desperately wanted to fit in somewhere. I also drank a lot. Alcohol and marijuana were the quickest and cheapest ways to medicate my hurting soul. They helped me forget the painful memories, the cutting words, the constant fear and the rough hands of my father.

There was something even more "magical" than alcohol or marijuana—sex. I used sexual activity to medicate the pain, heal my loneliness and escape the turmoil in my home. Of course, I wasn't really looking for sex. More than anything, my little girl's heart yearned for my father's safe embrace. I longed for something pure, straight and true. Daddies should always love their little girls but instead my father communicated a twisted, confusing lesson: love equals sex. So with an addictive hunger, I gave myself to men in an attempt to find real love (Woodley, 2013, p. 7).

Wow! This took me on a mind trip back to my high school years. For those of you who know me, personally, I may not have told you this but I am a recovering alcoholic. I have had experienced two major bouts with alcoholism, one when I was a teenager and the other in my early twenties, where I was considered a "functioning alcoholic"—that is, I was not able to function without at least two or three pints of rum a day; this may also explain why I do not like rum to this day. Well, when I entered East Orange High School in the fall of 1986, I was secretly harboring a lot of issues that go

121

beyond that of which a "typical teenager" sees at that age and stage of their life. By this time, I had experience a tremendous amount of loss and I had not really come to a healthy understanding of the meaning of so many (too many) things. For one, I had been bullied by several different people while in middle school, my self-esteem was shot, my parents split up and my dad died before they could reconcile, my biological father (my sperm donor) wasn't present in my life, and the list goes on. Oh, but, when I entered high school… I discovered a newfound freedom! My mom relaxed her tight grip a bit and allowed me to be more sociable and participate in several extracurricular activities. I quickly gained popularity like never before, but there was still a darker, sad side of me that many were not aware of until I was literally drunk every day.

My freshmen year was a year of adjustments and new beginnings, but by the time I was in the 10th grade things spiraled out of control. There were so many things going on back then that I really cannot remember them all. Well, as I said, I was in a lot of pain but I learned how to put on a happy face to hide my true feelings. What happened next nearly caused my emotional and mental bottom to fall out—I lost a cousin, an aunt and nearly lost my mother all in a span of 48-hours. My mom received a call from Bainbridge, GA with the news that her niece died, and then, her sister died shortly after. My mom was preparing to travel to Georgia the next day, but had a preaching engagement that Friday night. To make a long story short, I received the call from hospital telling me "You need to come to the University Hospital as soon as possible to *identify* Shirley Jones-Anderson." It turned out that my mother had a horrible car accident, where she nearly died. I was already an emotionally vulnerable child at that time, and to hear the word, "identify," that word was already associated with the call I received about the death of my dad a couple years earlier. It sent me into an emotional tailspin. And when she slipped into a coma...! Things got real! I found myself unraveling as evidence by me cussing at the nurses and the medical staff helping my mom, not sleeping, and most damaging, drinking a lot.

I found solace in an embracing friend named Bacardi Light Rum! It was like he called me by my name and promised to "take the edge off and help you to relax and sleep." I got this older guy to cop (purchase) a half pint for me one day after band practice and stuck it in my book bag to enjoy later. My brothers and I went to the hospital that afternoon, and again, I lost it. Roy, the second oldest, became so irritated with me that he sent my friend and I out of the room. I was so messed up that I convinced someone else to cop a pint of rum before I went in the house—forgetting that I already had a half-pint in my book bag. Oh the joy I experienced when I saw both of them laying side-by-side. Immediately, I hatched a plan: "I'll drink the pint tonight and the half pint in the morning." I was up to a pint in the morning and a pint-and-a-half in the evening before the end of that week. This went on for several weeks before someone took notice of my condition—Mr. Daryl Robinson, my band director, and La Keisha "Keisha" Blue, one of my closest friends.

No one really knew what was going on in my family's life nor how badly I suffered until Mr. Robinson and Keisha observed that I was clearly drunk nine something in the morning! Together, they pulled me into his office to see what was going on. After some time, I finally told them about what was going on and how my issues were affecting me terribly—"I drink because I can't feel nothing and don't want to." They devised a plan that would keep me from being alone too much. Mr. Robinson spent as much time as he could with me before going home to his family; and Keisha invited me to her house many days, where I until it was time to go to sleep. When I arrived home, which was not that far from Keisha's house, I was back at it again? I always kept a stash somewhere. Eventually, I was up to two to three pints of rum a day. This continued until Roy found out—or should I say was told—why I was always so calm. I came home expecting to climb in my bottle and it was missing. I tore that hiding place up looking for it. Roy, who was standing behind me, announced, "Looking for this?" He was holding my buddy in his hand. From then on, Roy joined Mr. Robinson's and Keisha's efforts to get me to straighten up. I made Roy promise me he would not tell my mom, that "I'll tell her when I'm ready." Needless to say, my reckless behaviors did not stop there. I was still doing favors, but by then, indiscriminately; and partying heavily. When I think back, some years later, I can see why folk said: "God surely looks out for widows and fools." God knows what could have happened to me during this first dark time in my life. My next fight occurred after I was sexually assaulted at the age of 22. This time I struggled alone for at least a year or so because I hid it from others so well.

Is That How you're Gonna Act?

Most of this section was taken from a project I completed following the painful ending of my second engagement in the fall of 2003. It is amazing how God will continuously allow certain conditions into our space until we learn from them and/or how to navigate through them. Allow me to open this section with a quote from Wilson

(1991):

> I'm suggesting that *you can't free it if you don't see it.* You cannot be free of your self-shaming until you knowingly choose to adopt a purposeful, temporary self-focus. I'm not saying we should spend our lives in introspective "navel gazing." We look *within* for the same reason we look *back*—to provide a context for change. In reality, our shame bound self-concepts affect us and our relationships with and others whether we know it or not (p. 90, emphasis mine).

One behavior that can develop as you continue to avoid emotional scars from your past can be summarized by what I call "shifty movements"—defense mechanisms one uses to manipulate people in most of the situations one is exposed to in their life. Some of the negative effects of using shifty behaviors are, they can easily become a part of your persona—who you are. Shifty movements can block you from exposing your true self to significant other(s), especially if your fear is experiencing rejection or even closeness. The driving force is fear, which is also rooted in shame. A good example that fits the shifty movements' description is my relationship with my second fiancée, Cindy. These behaviors developed in the way we engaged in our time together. As we started drawing closer to one another, we concealed many facets of our lives. Our manipulation brought about many problems. I still had not dealt with a number of my abandonment and distrust issues at the time, and they affected our relationship tremendously. In the end, I counted it as my fault. "I did it again," I thought, "I chased another woman off." I also said I was the one who did not love and trust freely. Lewis (1992) calls this kind of behavior "love withdrawal" (p. 9. 11). After arguing, discussing, and avoiding these issues, I realized Cindy and I shared similar issues. We mutually decided to separate to learn more about ourselves, share what we found in our moments of contemplation, and then learn how to be a friend to one another. But this plan did not materialize. "Love withdrawal, by its nature," Lewis (1992) contends, "is intense, thus making it difficult for the person affected to attend to the reason why the love was withdrawn. Love withdrawal leads to internal attribution of blame, and since it refers to the whole self—'I don't love you'—it also leads to global attributions of failure" (pp. 14, 15).

Acknowledging your weaknesses or shortcomings and how you function in them, and extend yourself in relationships, not only with people but also with God, is vital to your growth. One writer explained it this way, "It can be scary to lower your defenses and open up your life to others. When you reveal your failures, feelings, frustrations, and fear, you risk rejection... Vulnerability is emotionally liberating. Opening up relieves stress, defuses your fears, and is the first step to freedom" (Warren, 2002, p. 276). I can relate to this personally because I had to choose to do the work of releasing myself and taking the risk of exposing myself to Cindy, rather than trying hard to disguise my true self. I understood the benefits of doing so, no matter the outcome, would be worth the investment. I knew it was a great risk, but I had to give it a try. Not trying connotes fear; and this fear, this shame, literally tore us apart. Our bond could have been stronger if Cindy and I had been fully and truthfully present with one another as we shared with one another, regardless of the contents. It could have helped us to be our authentic selves around one another, if only we were both willing.

The more we used shifty movements by trying to avoid the sensitive areas of our lives, the more we participated in the perpetuation of distrust and deception; making for a relationship filled with suspicion, distrust and a lack of respect for one another. Wimberly's suggestive explanation for unmasking without fear of being abused fits this situation appropriately. He said, "People need to expose their true vulnerability and shame without fear of being exploited. Only in safe and secure relationships, in which the threat of exploitation of vulnerability is at a minimum, can the legacy of shame, be undone" (1999, p. 78). *Opening up to one another brings about mutual admiration, respect and love.*

We must do the same thing before God. Romans 14; 9, 10 says, "For to this end Christ both died, and rose and revived, that he might be Lord both of the dead and living. But dost thou judge thy brother [or sister]? For we shall all stand before the judgment seat of Christ" (*KJV*). If we cannot do this before God, we will not be able to do so with one another. There is nothing we can hide from God; therefore, we ought not to be ashamed when it comes to sharing with one another.

My untrusting, suspicious behaviors were rooted in that dreadful wintery night. Not only did I start drinking heavily again, I went from one toxic relationship to another. At first, life was good for me from the outset. I was an A/B college student, working two jobs, and was staying focused and out of trouble. And then, the incident happened and I started drinking to help keep both my thoughts at bay, and to maintain my state of denial. Only this time I was drinking a fifth of Bacardi's rum in a matter of a day or two. This was when I engaged in several unhealthy relationships.

One of the young women I "messed around with" was not a compatible match but we were sexually attracted to another. In that "relationship," we got together for sex only—no talking, no lunches, nothing but sex. This relationship ended with bang! We both took interest in someone else and did not say because we only talked enough to "hook up." Then, I started dating this girl with whom I was friends with her sister. She brought some scary things out of me, one being rage. One night we decided to go out separately. A friend from high school of mine invited me to their birthday party at a club I went to a lot back then, while my girlfriend hung out with her sister and their friends. I should not have gone out that night because I was already sick—I had been diagnosed with sarcoidosis (the inflammation of vital tissue organs) in my lower right lung the week before. The events that took place that night would have broke my mother's heart—I got arrested.

I was on powerful painkillers and they wore off sooner than they should have. I was serious pain while I was at the party. A good friend of mine was bartending that night and hooked me up and I did not pay for any of my drinks. It took quite a few shots to numb the pain let alone get me tipsy. So, me being the lush that I was, I kept drinking. I was able to have a good time that night—I was still a good dancer. My friends and I danced all night, in fact, we shut the place down. One of my other friends and her boyfriend, who lived near me, offered to give me a ride home. This "boyfriend" of hers was a member of a duo who had a popular club song out back then, and this song is still played today. Something about him rubbed me the wrong way. At first, I counted it to the fact that he was arrogantly flying high off the success of this song; but, I alarmingly discovered that was not it because I knew a number of successful artists at that time. Reluctantly, I agreed and got in the car with them. As the three of us drove along, this guy started to lose his temper quickly. He started yelling, cussing and threatening my friend. I remember thinking, "Aww shit! This is not good!" The next thing I knew he backhand slapped her across the face. Immediately, I demanded that he let me out of the car because we were not far from my house.

I really do not remember what happened next, but the car stopped and this guy pulled me out of the car, slammed me against the car—which caused the pain in my side to flare up sharply—and then, this fool punched me in the ribs on the side that was already hurting. This blow, combined with the pain I was already in, caused me to blackout. The next thing I knew I was sitting in the back of a police car with the platinum bracelets around my wrists. I stayed at the police station for a couple of hours because, believe it or not, my friend told the truth about her boyfriend attacking me and I was defending her and myself. I still had to go to court for this incident. When the summons arrived at my house and my mother retrieved it from the mailbox, I could have had a heart attack. I told her it was a jury duty notice. So I secretly went to this hearing without anyone knowing except someone close to me to whom I will not say right now, but I'm sure they will laugh when they read this.

It was during this hearing that I discovered what I had done and how much trouble I was in at that moment. As it turned out the arresting officer took pictures of the scene. When I saw them I did not recognize them until I saw a picture of my friends now ex-boyfriend, battered and bloodied. The arresting officer testified that "it appears that Mr. Jones flew into a rage and tried to put Mr. I-forgot-his-name's head through the windshield." I zoned out and cannot tell you what else was said until the judge snapped, "Mr. Jones!" If I never prayed before I did in those few seconds. The judge announced that he retrieved a copy of my college transcripts, spoke to my supervisor at one of my jobs, and did a criminal background check on me in preparation for this hearing. This made me relax a little but not really because the judge then said, "Under other circumstances this would be considered aggravated assault and battery, but because of all the mitigating factors—your school and work reports, and you do not have a criminal record—things are looking up for you. But before I render a sentence, tell the court what happened that night. And take your time and make it good." I swallowed so hard that it felt like a brick going down. I told the court about my recent diagnosis, the pain medication, the partying and the drinking to kill the pain, and the little bit that I remembered from the car. I recall my last words being something to this effect: "I have never done anything like this before. Even though I don't remember the fight, I am just as shocked as you are at the sight of those pictures…."

The judge and the courtroom fell quiet for what felt like an eternity. The judge stared at me intently, rubbing his temples for a few seconds. I could have peed my pants. Finally, the judge said in a voice that was much softer than it had been moments before, "I've been talking to some people about you before you arrived today. Your sentence will be probation with special stipulations. You will continue to attend Essex County College and work both jobs for the next 15 months. You will also meet with Dr. Anonymous and you two will come up with a plan that will help you to set a course for your educational future, while incorporating some courses that will include Abnormal Psychology, Criminal Justice and New Jersey Criminal law. Dr. Anonymous will introduce you to another professor, Dr. Psych and they will mentor you. You must also stay out of trouble until this time is up. And Mr. Jones, not even a ticket! Not a parking ticket, j-walking or anything! At the end of this 15-month probation, you and your mentors will appear before this court to report on your progress. If all goes well, I will expunge this charge from your record and this whole ordeal will be behind you." I stood there frozen, not knowing if I should have jumped up and down or cry. "And oh, by the way, Mr. Jones," the judge snapped, "I'm not finished with you yet." My thoughts raced, "Oh my God, he changed his mind!"

The judge went on a tear and leaned into me badly, but he was absolutely correct when he said the following (and I paraphrase, this took place over twenty years ago):

Mr. Jones, you know this was admirable but senseless act on your behalf? You could have killed or seriously injured that man? And for what? First, according to your testimony, you should have been home, recovering, studying, or doing something productive. Instead, you went out on medications and under your doctor's care, and you drank all night long. In reality, you could be held accountable for negligent actions. It is because you are normally productive in the community and you are pursuing higher education, and you don't have a record that you received the sentence you have. It could have been worse, and for what? If I see or hear of you getting in trouble before your 15-month probation is up it will be revoked and this issue will be revisited and considered in whatever you get into… Mr. Jones, it is this court's hope that you follow the stipulations to the letter. You have a bright future ahead of you, and there are things you will accomplish and you have no idea where you can and will go. See you in 15 months. God speed!

Two people I had never met before approached me as I stood at the defendant's table. It was Dr. Anonymous and Dr. Psych. They told me the judge asked them come to this hearing to support me. We immediately left the courthouse went to the school, which was across the street. These two stand-up, class act men talked to me for a couple of hours. As it turned out, Dr. Anonymous was a well sought after attorney and Dr. Psyche was a Criminal Psychologist. They decided to introduce me to one of their colleagues, who was also an attorney with a background in psychology—Dr. Linda. She was as tough as nails; in fact, she was much sterner than the two men. We devised a plan that would not only fulfill my court ordered stipulations, but "also put your ass on the path to academic success, and get you out of this school into the school that will suit your academic needs," Dr. Linda snapped.

For those who knew me back then, I hope this clears

up a lot of things that did not make sense, such as what took me so long to transfer to one of the 4-year colleges that accepted me for admission. The reason it took me so long to make up my mind on which school I would transfer to was because I was on probation, and could do so until I was finished with that. I do not have a record now because it was expunged in the summer of 1993, which also explains how and why I was able start studying at Kean College (now University) that fall. This explanation sounds like the reason Jesus shed His blood on Calvary—for the remission and forgiveness of our sins. I hope you understand and forgive me. My momma didn't raise me that way.

Chapter Ten:

It's about You

"This vision of freely held human agency has been a guiding principle in the lives of African Americans. It has been the metaphysical recognition of our power to be self-determining no matter the circumstances in which we find ourselves. Using power of soul, we find ways to self-actualize to be fulfilled. The power of soul fosters in us awareness that we must care the needs of our spirits and seek an emancipator spirituality. The soul's guiding light still shines no matter the extent of our collective blindness. At any moment, at any time, we can turn toward this light to renew our spirits and restore our souls"

bell hooks, *Rock My Soul* (2003, pp. 225 – 226)

I want to take some time to speak from my heart as I close Part Three and move onto the fourth and final part of this book. I opened this chapter with a powerful quote from bell hooks' *Rock My Soul*. This statement speaks to our ability to determine whether we *will* pursue a God-ordained direction for our lives or not, even after being mistreated and abused. Someone may be in a situation where he or she is filled with the stench of abuse and/neglect, and might feel powerless in changing it. You may have someone present in your life trying to help you by loving, empowering, enlightening and encouraging you; but for some reason, it does not seem to be working for you. You are so entrenched, engrossed, and used to your condition that a change in direction may seem almost impossible for you to see. I want to offer you the greatest news ever: The soul's guiding light still shines no matter the extent of our collective blindness. At any moment, at any time, we can turn toward this light to renew our spirits and to restore our souls. That guiding light that is shining is God's love, which is continuously reaching, extending, and offering a greater, refreshed purpose and direction for you to live in. It is time to shed the blinders of victimhood you have been wearing for so long to see and feel the warmth of God's radiant love. When you are ready, and only at that moment, will you begin to see God's truths for your life will become *FIRST NATURE*.

When you began to look at your past and the gory details therein, it is tempting to want to look away and/or put it on the back burner. In many instances, this is completely understandable because it takes time, energy, stamina and courage to face what occurred in your life. I understand how challenging this can be because, even today, I sometimes want to run away from what I know is an on-going process—healing, reviving, and adjusting. At any given moment, painful memories can flood my mind when I least expect it. When this happens, it sometimes hits like a ton of bricks. I can pray about it, reach out to someone I trust, or I slowly think those thoughts through. I am blessed, however, to have people who care enough to lovingly encourage me to press on. However, I do not want to make this appear as if it is easy for me to cope with all of the time. It took lots of therapy over the years, talking to others, and prayer to be able to deal with my feelings, for the most part.

I had the opportunity to explain my process to a good and trusted friend, and how these moments seem to get me to readjust, get back on track, and most importantly, find my way again. For me, these moments tell me something is off kilter. I have moments of anxiety, especially when it comes to people and things I care about. I become over-concerned about *their* stuff when I should not be. I tend to over-function on their behalf, instead of stepping aside. It drives them crazy until I realize what I am doing, and then, I become silent—almost dead silent. There are also times when I wrestle with bouts of depression. When this happens, as I explained to one of my godchildren, I can become verbally aggressive. Once I recognize my behavior, oftentimes I am able to reel myself back in, so to speak. I know my verbal aggression signifies several things are going on: I am unhappy for whatever reason, or I'm not feeling a person or situation, and I am trying to force them or make it to work. Sometimes I try to shake some sense into them or attempt to control the outcome because I do care about what is or is not happening. I can become so immersed in what I am pushing to accomplish that I use verbal aggression to intimidate or manipulate the person or the condition in the way I feel it, he or she should be. At some point, anxiety and/or depression sets in to let me know something is amiss, and I need to readjust by evaluating my actions and feelings—not their actions, feelings, or the environment's contents. This is not always easily done, but I have arrived at this place through years of paying attention to and learning myself. I do understand I cannot control everything and/or everyone in my life, even if it is painful to watch and my intentions are admirable. It takes an enormous amount of strength and courage for me to take my hands off of people and situations I really care about.

The principal aim for this brief chapter is to inspire, encourage, and empower you to take better care of yourself. Too many times, we treat ourselves the same or in a similar fashion that others are treating is now or have handled us in the past. We will neglect and ignore our own needs, put other people's needs before our own or simple wear our bodies down in a myriad of ways in order to avoid dealing with our own stuff. I'm not here to judge you because I do not always treat myself right. That, too, is a process for me— unlearning old conditionings and learning healthier ones.

In a perfect world there would be no need for empowerment over abuse and neglect; in that people would be considerate of others' needs, and there would be no use for punishing people for all types of brutality. But the upswing of this is that there are brave, faith-driven children of God, who are not ashamed of their testimony and are willing to share it with others. In doing so, I have had the opportunity to be exposed to different circumstances and achieving various levels of healing and maturation, which equipped me with not only the courage, but also the wisdom to know when and where to do so. I had to come to a place in my life where I am not ashamed of my story because it is not for me. That is the purpose of our stories and testimonies: They are for someone else to be healed and delivered from what they are experiencing in their lives. I have been told at least a million times or so, there is someone out there whose condition is worse than mine. If my story can help someone along the way, then I should share it. That is my same hope for you—only you have to come to a place where you are willing to open up and allow God's healing light of love to enter into your life. Yet there is some wisdom to this as well.

I have said years ago: You must come to a place

where the religious clichés that you use or hear so frequently actually means something in your life. In other words, those phrases are virtually meaningless until they can be applied directly to you or shed some light in your life. For example, I was involved in an accident with a truck in January 2004 as I was traveling back to Georgia from New Jersey after my father's funeral. I had always heard and said, "God looks after the widows and the fools." Well, I was the fool that night because I was driving in a terrible snow storm, hell-bent on getting back to Atlanta for work that Monday. It was foolish because I should have waited until the storm blew over. Instead, I tried to beat the storm and drove directly into it instead, and I had the wreck that Sunday night. Today, not only do I avoid driving in bad weather but I do not rush if I can help it. Therefore, I have learned to look at this saying, as well as many others, in light of my experience and where I believe God is taking me in my life and my ministry.

The same can be said about many of life's experiences and sharing your testimony. You must ask you yourself a few questions: How can I use my know-how to further the kingdom of God? Where can I draw the strength needed to do the will of God? How can I grow and benefit from the words I use to minister to those in need? Just thinking about these questions, and not necessarily having the answers to them, can help you along the way. Many times God gives us small glimpses into the future to motivate us enough to focus on God's will over our lives. I say *glimpses* because if we knew all of the details it might prove to be too much for our minds, and we might try to function without God or ahead of God's timing. This is also the case with the healing process as well. Healing oftentimes takes what feels like an eternity with many, many baby steps, and this does not include the setbacks and relapses. As they say, it's all a part of the journey, grist for the proverbial mill.

I am encouraged because I am hopeful that you will be able to participate in God's healing process in God's time for you. It cannot be forced or done when you want it to be done because it is the logical thing to do. The heart and the mind are not always on the same page nor do they also seek the same goal at times. It takes prayer, time, support and love to get into the position of progressive healing. Human nature is not always apt to change because it requires discomfort and stretching. The last thing the average person wants to feel is discomfort. Pain and suffering will be avoided at great lengths. Some people do not want to inflect or feel pain and end up causing more suffering than would have been initially felt. How unfortunate for all parties involved.

May God speed and bless you on your travels.

Part Four:

The Recovery

Chapter Eleven:

It's Okay to Be Empowered

<u>One Step at a Time</u>

One of the prominent feelings of a person whom had been violated, is the loss of control or feeling powerlessness over their body, and/or the situation they were in when the maltreatment occurred. This is an appropriate reaction in that it says something went wrong—"I was not in control of what happened to me." Whether it was earlier today, yesterday, or years ago, there is a sense of vulnerability regarding that situation. Some people try to convince themselves that "I've gotten over that" and "I've moved on from that," or from a religiosity perspective—that is an unreal or an unhealthy use of religion—"The Lord erased it from my remembrance." I do believe God can and will remove things from our hearts and minds; yes, I do. However, I am speaking of those individuals who had not been transformed or healed of the traumatic episodes in their lives. In other words, those whom are in denial over the situation they had experienced. Here's an example of what I am talking about: Think of that person whom you know whom had been abused, hurt, and/or traumatized. If within these conversations with them have a similar to their experience was broached, and their response is: "I'm blessed and highly favored," and you see or know it still hurts; that is whom I am referring to. "I'm blessed and highly favored" is a great affirmation to use but the problem is if that person still suffers from, wrangles with, and denies that their situation is real or that it had actually occurred, they are not healed. They are in denial in a major way. If this is you, I pray that you come to a place of acceptance, and an understanding of the purpose of that situation. The first step is to admit to yourself that something went wrong beyond your control, and you are not to blame for it occurring to you.

Admitting something happened that was beyond your control can be a taxing reality for some people. Many people do not like to own up to the fact that they lost control of a situation they were in. They might be considered "control freaks" or something like that, but for others it may be a heightened sense of shame for various reasons. For me, it was an ego thing, which was deeply rooted in shame. I did not want anyone to know, including myself, that I had been taken advantage of by a woman. So I suffered in silence for a while until I accepted the fact that I needed help. You must come to a point where you can acknowledge that something terrible has happened to you, and then, seek and accept help from others. Woodley (2013) wrote:

> You have to push against that feeling inside that makes you want to shut out everyone from your pain. Most of the time you'll want to run from the hurt. That's why you need someone who will hold your hand and be with you through it. The way to healing is with others, not without them. You've done that for far too long, trying to handle your sadness, shame and loss all by yourself.... (p. xviii).

Amen! Here is a biblical reference to make the

author's point clearer. In the book of Ecclesiastes, chapter 4: 7 – 12, writer said:

> I observed yet another example of meaninglessness in our world. This is the case of a man who is all alone, without a child or a brother, yet who works hard to gain as much wealth as he can. But then he asks himself, "Who am I working for? Why am I giving up so much pleasure now?" it is all so meaningless and depressing. Two people can accomplish more than twice as much as one; they get a better return for their labor. If one person falls, the other can reach out and help. But people who are alone when they fall are in real trouble. And on a cold night, two under the same blanket can gain warmth from each other. But how can one be warm alone? A person standing alone can be attacked and defeated, but two can stand back-to-back and conquer. Three are even better, for a triple-braided cord is not easily broken (p. 687, *NLT*).

There is a great sense of relief when you are able to release what is burdening you. Pray that God will show you someone you can trust and is willing support you and lend a hand as you pursue wholeness in your life. I found this to be true after years of holding onto a lot of emotional baggage, trying to figure it out on my own, and/or pretending it did not happen at all. But there is wisdom in trusting in someone during the tumultuous times of your life. Matsakis (1998) wrote of trusting someone in this powerful fashion:

In the midst of a trauma, friends are those you trust with everything including your life, and enemies are those you trust with nothing. Although there might be some people you aren't sure about or those who are trustworthy in some matters but not others, when you are living through a trauma, these kinds of fuzzy categories are useless. Hence, if someone is of questionable reliability, sheer survival may demand that person be seen as an "enemy." One of the most difficult problems trauma survivors have is learning how to adapt this all-or-nothing kind of thinking, that may have served them so well their trauma, to nontraumitic, everyday kinds of situations (p. 58).

I found this to be true in my own life because I was able to see its benefits. One day I blurted my experience out to my best friend, who, in turn, said, "I understand because I was abused for years." Something powerful happened in that moment: I gained lifelong companionship in my journey toward healing and so did my best friend. This did not start an on-going pity party. It added a powerful layer of accountability and support to our friendship. We support and encourage one another to remain on the path of our healing journeys regularly. Townsend (2011) supported this position when he wrote the following:

When you let someone know the nature of your hurt, you allow yourself to open up and be vulnerable. By telling another human being the facts and feelings about what you experienced, you give up the perception of being self-sufficient and emotionally impenetrable. In the presence of another, you acknowledge the reality that you suffered and receive support... Expressing weakness isn't just an emotional download; it has a twofold purpose. First, it brings your hurts out of isolation, where they would otherwise fester and make things worse. Second, it draws those hurts into a relational sphere, where care and support can repair the damage (pp. 62 – 63).

Some people say disclosure may not be the best thing for a "victim," and that person needs to "wait until the time is right for them." I agree wholeheartedly. Oftentimes, depending on the individual, talking about a traumatic incident prematurely can have devastating consequences in that the person may be scarred psychologically and/or emotionally, which could alter the course of their life. So, I strongly agree with not pressing the individual to tell their story when they are ready to do so on their own. However, I do believe a person should be encouraged to face what has happened to them in order to help them avoid the development of suppressive behaviors—where the individual "pushing" emotions down by avoiding them rather than dealing with them in a healthy way. In fact, Greenberg (2011) explained this phenomenon in the following:

Transformation of distressed feelings begins with attending to the aroused feelings (e. g., "I feel bad") followed by exploring the cognitive-affective sequences of that the bad feelings (e. g., "I feel hopeless," What's the use of trying?"). Eventually this leads to the activation of some core maladaptive emotion schematic self-organizations based on fear or shame (e. g., "I'm worthless," "I can't survive on my own"). At this point in the transformation process a

145

new adaptive experience is accessed (p. 83).

Moreover, I also believe it would be helpful if he or she would let someone—a trusted friend or loved one—know what's going on with them, while firmly expressing their need to talk about it when he or she is able, both emotionally and mentally. "I'm going through something right now and I will talk more about it when I am ready," is all that is needed. This can motivate the supportive, trusted friend or loved one to uphold accountability in the person who was treated badly. The trusted friend can also help the other person avoid being caught up in making excuses (avoidance) as to why they are not moving toward acceptance and healing. If he or she seems to be trapped in the "when I get ready" mode for a long time, the caring person can remind them that they need to face their situation and/or seek help to address what they may be feeling, even as they stall and avoid what is occurring in the heart and in their mind. Dealing with your feelings can help relieve some of the emotional pressure mounting in your life. Believe it or not, this is not a sign of weakness but a great step toward empowerment!

Now That the Cat's Out the Bag!

Now that you have told a trusted loved one about your harrowing experience, and you are preparing to gr address what occurred in your life, I have an effective exercise for you in the meantime—journaling. For some, this can serve as a cathartic (therapeutic, cleansing) channel to which your raw emotions can be expressed in a safe, creative way. For others, journaling might appear to be a chore to which they are not willing to maintain. In my experience of mentoring and counseling others, journaling proved to be effective in preparing them for the therapeutic process in that he or she was able to start the conversation and was able to verbalize his or her feelings without having to work as hard in understanding the emotions he or she felt.

Sometimes the journaling process can be effective without having to commit to a therapeutic relationship with a counselor or therapist. This is how it worked with my first female mentee. I would come up with questions and she answered them by writing entries in her journal. I gave her a certain amount of time to complete her entries, and then, she would give me the journal to read and I offered feedback. We had two to three journals circulating between us so she would not be without a journal to either answer additional questions or to write about whatever she felt like sharing.

The journaling, like the therapeutic process, takes time to develop into an open exchange between the parties because it requires trust for the person to openly write about certain aspects of their life. The person writing the entries might do what is also typical in the therapeutic setting—use avoidance tactics and other defense mechanisms until he or she is ready to write freely. However, once trust is established, "Expressive coping," one writer said, "also may help one attend to and clarify central concerns and may serve to promote pursuit of goals," (Greenburg, 2011, p. 75) which I would presume is also helping him or her to achieve healing and wholeness.

I strongly suggest that rules and boundaries be established at the beginning of this process, and that both parties repeatedly discuss certain facets of the journaling process. Both persons should be able to talk to one another as well. This can help alleviate confusion and/or disconnect in the question and answer portion of their written exchanges. The person writing questions might feel that their questions were clearly written, while the person reading and responding to them may not understand what the other person is asking of them. Further clarification will be needed. They should be able to dialogue for clarity on an ongoing basis as to how the process is progressing—whether regression, stalling, or stagnation is occurring. Both parties should also discuss the expectations of this process, and talk about how this process can be improved in order to precede efficiently.

I used this journaling process with another female mentee years after I used it with my first female mentee. Initially, I insisted that she see a therapist I knew could help her figure some things out in her life. She vehemently resisted because she did not want to "talk to a stranger," and that she "trusted" me and asked me to help her as much as I could. We agreed to go forward with the journaling process using the same format as I used with the other female mentee. As anticipated, there was a lot of avoidance, confusion, and clarifying. These were stalling tactics in that she believed I would not press her to get into deep places of her heart. A lot of time and energy went into trying to get her to open up and write freely. We started this process because she had an episode that required immediate attention, but we soon arrived at a place of frustration and resistance.

After a couple of months of writing and poising questions, reading the responses, and rephrasing and presenting the same questions in several ways, several times, she seemed to have been in a state of impasse—where things were not moving, even though she continued to answer the questions. This was frustrating me because, knowing this person somewhat, I was aware of how and when she was avoiding the questions. I offered feedback to encourage her to "say more," and the same thing—just enough to say something was written. I realized my irritation was really my transference (when the person helping the other places their feelings on the other person) and that my mentee was not willing to fully participate in the process, even though it was for her benefit. I really wanted to help her, but her responses regarding the status of her entries were, "Oh, it's coming along." It was her passive-aggressive way of not wanting to address her needs, but to appease me. However, this process cannot be an effective tool if both parties are not willing or ready to participate openly, in a committed fashion. Therefore, I advised her that writing the entries must "be something you want to do in order for this process to work for *you*." The challenges we experienced can be understood in Lewis' (1995) words when he discussed "the shame command" in the following:

> ....it is about self, not about action; thus, rather than resetting the machine toward action, it stops the machine. Any action becomes impossible since the machine itself is wrong. The shame interruption is more intense given the identity of the subject-object. That the violation involves the machine itself means, functionally, that all behavior ceases its function, then, is to signal the ***AVOIDANCE*** of behaviors likely

cause it. Its aversiveness functions to ensure conformity to the standards and rules. While shame, more than guilt, should be likely to change behavior, thought, or feeling, its averseness may be so extreme that shame is bypassed. If bypassing occurs, a shame state may be ineffective in producing a change in behavior (p. 35, emphasis mine).

Once the journaling process moves along, I suggest that discussions about what was written occur from time-to-time, because there may be some powerful phrases or disclosures contained in these entries and responses (feedback) that will not have the same value as they would in the face-to-face exchange. Something miraculous happens when people interact with one another. It's called *INTAMCY*. At this stage, the trusted friend or loved one can act as a sponsor (one who prays for/with and listens to the other person, even as certain aspects of the story may be repeated often). I also suggest that the trusted person keep a journal or a log of what is addressed in order to help the other person to remember what was said and written during the journaling process—this is a part of the accountability portion of the relationship. When a person is allowed to, given permission to, and encouraged to speak and/or write freely, he or she can start to work through the pain, anger and the shame as they prepare to start a therapeutic relationship with a counselor or therapist, or continue to progress on their trek toward wholeness. This was helpful for me, personally. There were times when I needed to make adjustments in my life and trusted friends were available to listen to and discuss with me some of my thoughts and feelings. Talking it out as well as journaling still helps me to sort things out. If this does not do the trick, I know how to call my therapist friend to schedule a session or two.

150

What Next?

Let's say the person who experienced trauma and/or maltreatment had divulged what has happened to them to a trusted friend or loved one and is fully engaging in a cathartic release (i.e., journaling, or other creative activities), and is able to actively talk about their feelings, what is the next step? This can be tricky because the person whom has been the supportive friend should begin encouraging the other to explore seeking professional help and guidance, if this is necessary. This has to be done carefully without stirring up feelings of abandonment, rejection or any other negative feelings he or she experienced in other relationships that caused them extreme pain.

By this time, the relationship between the supportive person and the emotionally vulnerable person may have grown stronger because there has been a lot of information exchanged as well as emotions along the way. Encouraging the person to decide if professional intervention may be a necessary step in their growth and healing, could be healthy for both parties involved. Additional assistance may be appropriate in that the emotionally injured person may have developed mental or emotional conditions that are beyond the supportive person's reach. Seeking additional help can also reduce co-dependency amongst the two persons. Engel (2006) called this occurrence enmeshment—wherein "an unhealthy dependence on another person" (p. 107). It is important that both people understand that seeking professional help may not be the end of their relationship. I advocate that for both parties to continue to engage one another because their relationship can prove to be lifelong and beneficial for them both.

An experienced counselor or therapist can bring an objective eye to the situation that may not be achieved by the trusted friend or loved one. The counselor or therapist can be effective in that he or she is not personally invested in what brings the person into the therapeutic relationship. What this means is that the counselor or therapist can be interested in the person and compassionate toward their needs, but he or she is not personally connected like a friend or a family member would be. The counselor or therapist will also be able to provide other useful skills and resources that the trusted individual may not be aware of. He or she can also offer pertinent questions for the journaling process to which the person and their trusted friend can use as the journaling process continues.

The counselor or therapist can also facilitate, coach and teach coping skills as the emotionally susceptible person encounter circumstances that cause them to experience extreme emotional and mental distress. Certainly, the trusted friend can be a support during those challenging moments; however, the therapist or counselor can help to process, work through, and make sense of what being felt and/or thought at the time. One method I have used while assisting clients during emotional crises is like counting backwards. First, I start by having the person to verbally identify what is felt or thought at that moment. This helps him or her to focus and regain composure of his- or herself, which involves them making "I feel" statements to describe their thoughts and feelings. Next, I would encourage them to explain how or what brought them to their moment of distress. Not only does this help him or her to calm down, eventually, but it also causes him or her to reconnect to the logic or critical thinking aspect of their being. This technique can also help him or her to identify triggers they may not have been aware of before this incident. And then, I assist him or her in the processing (working through by thinking and speaking about) what had transpired. This can be repetitive and arduous at best, but it should be expected because healing takes some effort and time for it to take roots a person's life.

I would also suggest that the traumatized person join a group of people who had experienced similar situations, and are learning to adjust and live in the aftermath of their traumatic event. One of the greatest adversaries of this healing process is one's pride, which could be rooted in shame. As mentioned earlier, a person can easily fall into the trap of self-reliance ("I can do this all by myself"), and suffer longer than they have to. By joining a support group, you will find that you are *not* alone in what you had experienced, how you feel, and how you view yourself following your traumatizing event(s). There are too many people suffering from this self-reliant mentality, some come out of it while others tend to loiter in it out of habit. For the ones who came out of it, they may be able to assist you in ways that your trusted friend or therapist may not be able to due to their lack of personal experience of situations similar to those you may have endured. What is important is that you understand that you do not have to travel on your journey towards healing alone. I have heard many, many times before, "healing does not take place in a vacuum." And it doesn't. It takes several parts working together toward a common goal: Wholeness and fulfillment.

Take It and Run With It

Do you believe you are loved by others, even if they do not know you personally or have ever not met you face-to-face? Can you feel the sincere compassion emanating from the pages of this book? Do you believe God still has a hand on your life even when it feels as though you are damaged goods? I genuinely believe this book was inspired by God because in most cases in the past I would not have talked about my experience let alone write a book. I may not know you or have heard your story; I still care about what becomes of you. I love you enough to share my story, some of what I had experienced as a mentor/counselor/therapist, as well as personally. I will also share some of the methods and techniques I have had access to over the years I have utilized professionally and personally.

Read and meditate on the words of Revelation 12: 11, which says, "And *they overcame him* by the blood of the Lamb, and by *the word of their testimony*; and *they loved not their lives unto the death*" (KJV, emphasis mine). Awesome! What does this mean in this context? Let's start with "they overcame him." How? They, the angels, acted by obeying the commands of God and they fought the dragon. They slew the dragon and were victorious through the blood of Jesus, which is the Lamb. This can be done in your life as you plead the blood of Jesus over your circumstances. God will show you who, how, when and why as you go forward on your journey toward healing and wholeness. Once I opened my mouth to my best friend about what happened in my life, it was not by chance or a decision I made on my own. God ordered it and brought it to fruition through our obedience. I could have continued to rely on figuring it out for myself, but instead, God placed people in my life to help, support and encourage me along the way. Even though some of these people are no longer with me physically, I can still use what they gave me as I live.

Next, is "the word of their testimony…." They were able to share their experiences with others based on what they accomplished by the blood of the Lamb (Jesus). Whenever you hear the saints singing: "I tried Him and I know. Found Him to be a friend. I know too much Him. On Him I can depend…," (Elbertina Clark Terrell, 2007) they are most likely declaring their experience with going at something with the help of Jesus or the blood of the Lamb; thereby, sharing their testimony with others. Nothing can be more powerful than hearing how a person was in a precarious situation, looking for a way out, and then, giving it to Jesus, who walked with and helped them out of whatever betides them. This can and will be you! Focus on the above verse.

And, finally, "they loved not their lives unto the death…." This is and can be inspirational as one doubts or questions why certain things happened to them: The "why me" moments that many experience throughout their journeys. Remember this: your experiences in life are not always about you. They are for others. So whenever you ask the question, "Why me?" Think of this response: "Why not me?" God has a plan for your life that no one else can carry out. I am a living witness that God, in God's infinite wisdom, crafted a path for our lives that no one else can walk out. Yes, even those dreadful moments of abuse and trauma! All of these things are designed for God's glory (Romans 8: 28). Someone once asked me: "How can you believe God would allow some of the most evil things in this world to transpire, even to His faithful children?" Well, my answer was and is, even though it took quite some time for me to arrive there, "All things work together for the good of those who love the Lord, and are called according to His purpose" (Romans 8: 28)!

* * * * *

It is time to get into methods portion of this book in order to promote and assist you in your healing journey. This is the portion of this process I have been anticipating, but I had to get through the emotional stuff first. I am so *excited!* So let's press on.

Chapter Twelve:

Accountability: Let's Walk Together

Because I am a Christian Counselor and Therapist, from this point forward, many portions of Part Four will speak from a Christ-centered, therapeutic point of view; meaning, I will be speaking as a therapist/counselor, who is also Christian. I would like to state my perspective in regards to assisting others in the healing process following sexual trauma(s). My supposition is that people who have endured the shock and the trauma of sexual violence are in need of emotional, mental, spiritual healing and recovery more so than physical healing. Our bodies will heal long before our hearts, spirits, and minds. Therefore, I believe incorporating methods, techniques, and practices that seek to address the above stated parts of our beings is needed and necessary to restore wholeness.

<u>Emotionally Alert</u>

Once a person willingly enters the therapeutic setting and begins establishing a relationship with a counselor or a therapist, he or she will begin a cycle that is not always followed in a specific order. John entered this setting eager to begin the process, for example, and then, he started shutting down emotionally by the third session of the process. By the fourth session, John avoids many of the therapist's questions and remarks. He continues this behavior during the next two sessions, but is rejuvenated by the next session. He returns to his original enthusiastic self, ready to face his "demons" (issues that brought him into this relationship in the first place).

Looking to Greenburg's (2011) concept of the "Phases of Treatment" presented in her book, *Emotion-Focused Therapy*, I will discuss the therapist's role in the therapeutic process and how he or she should strive to develop and preserve the helping relationship with the person seeking help. After years of trying to find an approach that suits my style for helping others, Greenburg's "Phases of Treatment" makes plain as to how I set out to establish and maintain a therapeutic relationship. "EFT (Emotion-Focused Therapy) treatment has been broken into three major phases, each with a set of steps to describe its course over time" (Greenberg & Watson, 2006; in Greenberg's 2011). The three phases this author referred to are—"The first phase of bonding and awareness is followed by the middle phase of evoking and exploring. ...a transformation phase..." (Greenberg, 2011, p. 82). Greenberg continued on to explain these phases in the following:

> The first phase, bonding and awareness, involves four steps: (a) attending to, empathizing with, and validating the client's feelings and current sense of self; (b) providing a rationale for working with emotion; (c) promoting awareness of internal experience; and (d) establishing a collaborative focus. The second phase, evoking and exploring, also involves four steps: (a) establishing support for emotional experience, (b) evoking and arousing problematic feelings, (c) undoing interruptions of emotion, and (d) helping the client access primary emotions or core maladaptive schemes. The final

phase, generating new emotions and creating new narrative meaning, involves three steps: (a) generating new emotional responses to transform core maladaptive schemes, (b) promoting reflection to make sense to experience, and (c) validating new feelings and support an emerging sense of self (p. 82).

I was excited when I first read this description because it really helped me to reconsider some of the methods I had been using, and it also filled in some blanks as well, especially in the bonding and awareness phase. I talked about some of the challenges I experienced with one of my mentees. When she and I agreed to participate in the journaling process to help her to work through some of the emotional challenges she had been experiencing, it seemed like a great idea at first. Earlier on in the process it seemed as if we got stuck in an impasse wherein she seemed to have been avoiding the questions presented to her, and, at times, used deception to hide her true feelings about participating in *her* journaling process openly and honestly, even though it was designed to help her to release, if you will, what was causing her periodic emotional turmoil. I was aware of some of the events from her past that may have contributed to her suffering, but she was not ready to address those challenges. Her passive-aggressive refusal to buy into the process frequently led to confusion and exasperation, and trust issues developed between us. Therefore, the bonding phase that was to be established, cultivated, and maintained was strained, and this undertaking hit a major snag. In retrospect, my assessment of the challenges my mentee and I experienced in her journaling process was that she may have agreed to participate because of our existing relationship, but she did not truly feel that her situation warranted positive attention.

It did not help that I was also involved in several other children's lives, and I may have been a bit hasty in trying to get the process moving. In the end, this type of journaling undertaking may have been too much for her, emotionally, and for me.

In order for the journaling process to have been productive for my mentee there were several things that were needed in order to have given her the impression that her feelings were validated. I could have related to (or empathized) what she needed to express; but instead, she may have felt as though I joined in with others whom she felt were mistreating her. In hindsight, if the individuals who were identified as the perceived maltreators were observed and/or conveyed, this may not have been an issue to begin with. This may have been her excuse for not achieving true bonding. To achieve the first step of bonding and awareness, one party cannot be responsible doing the work or overworking. It can only occur by the actions of both parties. One cannot bond with another without him or her rising to the level where he or she is willing to inform the other of what hurts them and why and so forth. With my mentee, my job was to attend to whatever she wanted to tell me, and then, validate her feelings. If I was not made aware of certain situations and how they affected her, there was no way for me to know what was occurring, apart from sitting back and observing her interactions with the other individuals. Not disclosing this information created conditions where opportunities for attendance were missed and shame was felt and fortified, and, therefore, a strained relationship was the result. Although the reasoning behind the journaling exercise was designed to benefit my mentee, she passively agreed to continue, even though she was not emotionally prepared or willing to commit to this process wholeheartedly. Therefore, it did not work out the way it was intended to because there was no real sense of how she felt about various settings and people.

Yet my mentee's journaling process was salvaged by us reconnecting and carefully walking through the latter steps of the first phase—the essence of our relationship and the rationale for continuing on with the journaling process (bonding and awareness). I also gave her the power and the control to identify the areas to which she wanted address; thereby, an agreeable focus to which the process would proceed. By addressing the shame experienced within the situation in which she believed I sided with those whom she felt were mistreating her was actually the basis for not only the foundation by which we started anew, we reached an amenable focus to which the journeying process would go on from that point.

It is important to remember that there is a negative impact that occurs when a person has experienced an emotional disturbance—there was a loss of trust. Matsakis (1998) explained this loss as: "Trauma is about loss, and one of the first causalities of having been traumatized is the capacity to trust, especially if your trauma truly involved human evil or error," (p. 57). Trauma robes people of their innocence and faith in that they are exposed to conditions they may not have been aware of before. Matsakis continued on to say:

Trauma survivors not only lose trust in some of the

basic premises that keep people functioning (such as the assumptions of personal invulnerability and that the world is just and fair) but they can also lose trust in people, including themselves. "To trust, or not to trust?" is the question trauma survivors ask most frequently. "I want to trust, but I know better,' is the usual reply…. If you've been traumatized, you probably have good reason not to trust others. Your list of personal betrayals may be extensive, and quite devastating. If you trusted others during your trauma and they let you down, their failures to do as they had promised didn't result in the mere loss of a few dollars or a few hours of your time. Their failures may have put your life at risk, damaged you permanently, or cost the lives or health of others (p. 57).

Supposing the steps of phase one were laboriously achieved, as they should have been, then step two or the "middle" phase of evoking and exploring should have started with a higher degree of focus and commitment. By carefully using some of the elements experienced during phase one should make the evoking and exploration of the feelings my mentee felt during that "hurt-filled" moment led to her to seeking to take her journal and in our verbal dialogues seriously. Thus this was the basis for motivating my mentee to recommit to this process both mentally and emotionally because she wanted and needed to take advantage of a beneficial process that would give her a healthy outlet for the negative emotions she felt. It also motivated us to want to form a bond that was genuine and sincere.

Tamar's Healing

* * * * *

Let's face it, healing from traumatic events in our lives is very difficult because there will be many times when we must face a lot of emotions and feel the pain. Yet, within this process a large number of wonderful things can be achieved. Although the pain of some things we experience in our lives may never go away, we can convert them into useful, productive memories, whenever it is possible. Take the loss of a loved one, for example. The focus on the loss can be shifted toward pleasant, happy memories as a means to soothe one's self. The question can be asked: Can this be achieved in instances such as rape or sexual abuse? I believe it can be, although there is nothing happy about being violated in such a horrific way. Another meaning or feeling can be assigned to this experience that would give the individual some sense of relief, especially during and after a devastating episode was experienced.

In the pages of this book, my goal is to not only inspire you to walk on as you seek to obtain God's healing for your life, but also minister to others. When I say minister I do not mean this in the popular, traditional sense of delivering the Word, evangelizing, or missionary work. What I do mean is as you seek God's will in your life, ask for God's direction so that you can discover what it is God would have you to do in someone else's life. This may mean being present with them, holding their hand, or giving them information as to how to find help for themselves. Remember: Healing is not achieved in a vacuum. People need people in the healing process. You are not alone in your suffering and you are not alone in your healing.

Chapter Thirteen:

Tamar's Healing Is Found in Jesus:

Addressing What Matters

"Iron sharpens iron, and one person sharpens the wits of
another."

Proverbs 27: 17 (*NRSV*)

"Keep alert, stand firm in your faith, be courageous, be
strong. Let all that you do be done in love."

1 Corinthians 16:13 – 14 (*NRSV*)

Finally, I have arrived at the place where all of the
aforementioned discussions will come together because
shame and sexual abuse/trauma are *serious* matters. By the
time this chapter and the epilogue ends, I would have prayed
that God would have continued to guide me in the direction
God sees fit for this book, I had read the last round of books
ordered, and prayerfully mapped out a functional method for
my counseling practice: Tamar's Healing—kinda catchy, isn't
it? One word of caution: This chapter will be lengthy.

I Belong To You

I purposefully chose the above biblical verses and the
subtitle because it is time to bring this writing project to a

wonderful crescendo, and then, an end. Saying this phrase should ring musically in your ears: "I belong to you..." Say it a few times. A smile should begin bubbling up inside of you. I started this section this way because I will present two people who felt as though they were not wanted. People who harbor these types of feelings are emotionally volatile and can be dangerous in that they can be unintentionally erratic and hurtful; yet, at the same time, there's hope for them.

The first person is a young man who called himself "a throw away." When explaining what he meant by such a harsh description of himself, this young man said, and I quote, "Because every time I think somebody loves me and want to be around me, I end up hurt. Every time I decide to open up and let somebody in, they toss me to the side like a piece of trash." Listening to this young's man story was heart-wrenching. In a way, it made me angry because this teen demonstrated hope in humanity time after time, and was devastated repeatedly. He came to me because someone told him, "Dr. Jones has hope for young people. Go talk to him." I continued talking with this gentle spirit, enclosed in the body of this tormented man-child. He yearned to remain true to who he was created to be but the people around him reinforced the poisonous message: You are only good for this or that. A month after meeting with him, this young man began to see that he was not who *they* said he was, but he had something especially unique inside his being—"God didn't make me to be like them, God wants me to do something. Now I have to figure out what it is," he announced. It was refreshing to hear this epiphany.

There was a young woman who said, "Nobody really wants me," and desperately wanted to be near those she felt rejected her. She wanted them to accept her and did many things to get their attention—any attention, whether it was good, bad, indifferent, negative, or positive. It did not seem to matter, as long as it was attention, she had to have it. One day, someone noticed what she was doing to herself, how she was creating more and more damage to her own spirit. This person stepped in to minister to the young woman out of love, to sharpen her out of love when no one else cared enough to do so. The younger woman ended up turning against her by treating this person worse than those she felt did not want her. Although this younger woman did reframe from some of the behaviors that caught the woman's attention, she soon returned to them once she started feeling better about herself. What this younger woman did not know is that she lost someone who really saw something great in her and wanted to see her shine. Distrust developed and that person did as Jesus instructed his disciplines as he sent them off on a missionary assignment: "If anyone will not welcome you or listen to your words, shake off dust from your feet as you leave that house or town" (Matt. 10: 14, *NRSV*). The woman distanced herself from the young woman; even though this was "one of the hardest things" she ever had to do. However, this was the best thing she could do because the boundaries within that relationship had already dissolved and it was becoming dangerously unhealthy for the both of them.

Both instances were very unfortunate. One wanted to belong to someone, he wanted to be loved but those around him would not love him the way he deserved to be loved; while, on the other hand, the other had someone's love and she rejected it. Why do they do that? That's where I will go next—the family and the individual, him- or herself. Although we are brought up and socialized within a family unit, ultimately, it is up to the individual to seek and find Tamar's healing, which is found in Jesus the Christ. Once again, I will be writing from a Christian Counselor/Therapist's perspective. So here we go!

We Are Family

When I say family, what does this mean to you? Is it composed of a mother, father, and children? Or does it go beyond this narrow scope? Whatever your definition of family is, family can play a vital role in your healing process. Let us keep in mind what the premise of this book is: Healing the shame that follows sexual trauma. As I move forward, I will continue to link the meanings, roles, and functions of the family into the healing of shame brought on from a shame-filled event. Let's look at some ways family is defined. The *Merriam-Webster's Collegiate Dictionary and Thesaurus* (2007) defines family in the following manner:

> 1: a group of individuals living under one roof and under one head: HOUSEHOULD 2: a group of persons of common ancestry: CLAN 3: a group of things having common characteristics; especially: a group of related plants or animals ranking in biological classification above a genus and below an order 4: a social unit usually consisting of one or two parents and their children (p. 291).

Smith's (2007) definition of family also incorporates

the effects/affects that fit into the context of this book, when she wrote:

> Family is a part of a group of people related by heredity. It is also the most important and unique of human relationships. Family is the structure that *should* provide love, comfort, companionship and security. When the family has a strong structure, it produces strong families with the parents as role models, raising better children, and they all make a positive contribution in their community. The opposite is apparent with the disruption of the family when traumatic events occur within this structure. One such traumatic occurrence is sexual assault. Sexual assault is a frightening, traumatic and life-threatening experience which disrupts every aspect of a rape victim's life. This traumatic event that affects one member of the family can affect every other member. Family members react when their loved one has been violated; it is upsetting to watch them go through this ordeal. A family may experience some of the same effects as the victim, such as: denial, anger, shock, disbelief and feelings of helplessness... (p. 55, emphasis mine).

This description is unique in that it speaks to the distinguishing characteristics of the family's role in the life of person who experienced sexual abuse or assault. Many times, the family members are in need of help understanding and processing what has happened to their family member just as much as the person who experienced the assault. This can be seen in how the person's family members respond to what has occurred. Their reactions and responses may determine how the person will behave—resistance or progression in the healing process. Wimberly (1999) explained it this way: "There are, indeed, many social and interpersonal forces helping us resist moving into the future and letting go of certain destructive patterns" (p. 28). Remaining in the state of denial, for example, can lead to other behaviors that will allow the person who was traumatized to mask or cover their shame and create additional emotional and/or mental challenges. This is learned and reinforced within the family, especially if they, themselves, are shame-based individuals. Yet, Wimberly continued on to explain the family's role by using the family systems theory in the person's situation when he wrote the following:

> Family systems theory emphasizes that there is constant feedback from the environment to which the individual and family must respond. The family needs to face this feedback with its internal mechanisms operating and incorporate new information in ways that enable each family member to grow and develop. Healthy families function on positive feedback in that they process in ways that enhance the growth of all of its members. Unhealthy families, however, view feedback negatively and resist taking in new information, particularly if new information challenges existing family patterns. Dysfunctional families conspire with individual family members to resist change and hold on to current patterns of interaction. *Not knowing the future, such families prefer the present* (pp. 28 – 29, emphasis mine).

Within a family that is comprised of shame-based

individuals, some, if not all of them, may push to keep things hidden by filtering new information. New information, such as sexual assault or rape, may to be too much for these family members to cope with and, therefore, the shame-based family members will want to cover it up and *not* deal with the pain, shame, and the recovery that the individual will need to process in order to heal. This can be a hindrance to the traumatized individual. In situations like this, the individual oftentimes think of others when he or she should be thinking of themselves. His or her shame and guilt may be heightened in that they do not want to cause further damage to others by moving forward, which entails acknowledging that he or she was sexually violated. Holcomb & Holcomb (2011) explained these feelings in the following:

> Unfortunately, it's not uncommon for less than gracious responses to come from family and friends. When this happens, feeling of guilt are compounded. In addition, police, doctors, nurses, detectives, lawyers, or social workers may reinforce a victim's feeling that she or he "asked for it." Many victims believe that they could have or should have resisted more forcefully. The question of "why could I not stop the assault? or the belief that "if I had only been smarter, stronger, or braver maybe it wouldn't have happened to me" intensifies the sense of guilt...
> ...many victims feel guilty for embarrassing their family and community by opening up about their abuse and reporting it to the police. In some communities there exists a "culture of silence" whereby talking about sexual assault, reporting perpetrators, or air "family business: burdens victims even further (p. 109).

These authors presented a good position regarding the person in distress; however, I do not agree with many of their points. In my opinion, many of the feelings the distressed person experiences in such situations within his or her family and community lean more toward feeling shame rather than guilt—in that shame is a feeling and guilt is the result of an action. When a person has been sexually violated, he or she did not commit the violation, they were violated. Therefore, they feel the effects of the aftermath of this traumatic event. However, Holcomb & Holcomb (2011) did astutely follow-up by saying:

> If any of the above-mentioned feelings accurately portray your experience, it is very important for you to know that the assault was not your fault. The offender is guilty, not you. Nothing you did was "asking for it" and while you may feel guilty because you believe you could have somehow avoided the experience by acting differently, the offender is always at fault, never the victim (p. 110).

Living in environmental conditions such as these, the traumatized person can be re-traumatized repeatedly without actually knowing it. The unfortunate aspect of these surroundings and behaviors is that family members do not realize what they are doing—my hope is that they do not. Once again the person's family may begin hiding certain things. Stone (2004) explained these hiding and secret keeping phenomena this way:

Family therapist Nancy Boyd-Franklin writes that there are two kinds of secrets: those that are kept from outsiders but are known by most family members, and those that are kept from other family members. The first type is an open secret, generally known but not discussed. The second is a form of deception. Secrets can live for generations just behind a family's façade.... Keeping abuse an open secret within the family not only fails the survivor and excuses the abuser's behavior, but also strains relationships within the family and without. In many cases people don't know what to do when they see or hear that one of the clan is an abuser. If they believe (which family alliances and politics may keep them from doing), they're shocked, disgusted, and embarrassed. Extended family members thank their luck states it wasn't them or their kids. And then they keep it to themselves. This kind of denial—knowing something happened, but not acknowledging it—devastates a survivor (p. 59, also contains Boyd-Franklin, 1989.)

The above explanation may demonstrate why the traumatized person's family may be in need of intervention as well. I mentioned earlier that the family unit may contain shame-based individuals, because there is a reason why he or she is shame-based and they may have been hiding it for quite some time. Why is that? This would be the most logical question to ask. The above quote mentioned that secrets can live for generations, and so does the behavioral patterns. In the many religious and spiritual circles, these are called generational curses which simply means behaviors, attitudes, ailments, etc. that are passed down from generation to generation. It's important to understand what makes people shame-based individuals. There are some families out there where sexual abuse and immorality has not missed one generation dating back as far as that family can remember. When these and other events are hidden, covered up, and kept away from others for fear of being "found out," then they become and behave based on the shame they live and feel. Therefore, when it occurs within the current or next generation, the elders are not surprised and may say, "He or she will be alright;" and this becomes a part of the family's secrets.

Find another Way Out

What can a person do if they are a member of a toxic, shame-based family unit? This can be one of the most heart-wrenching, compelling, and difficult decisions an individual can make because it may call for drastic measures. My best advice to you is: *You will have to decide if you are going to continue living in your family's legacy of abuse and secrets or find another way out—differentiate.* When you decide to differentiate, this simply means you are willing to do things differently from the rest of your family or inner circle. It is outside of your inner circle you will have to find people who have achieved the goal you are trying to attain—pulling away from one's family and inner circle to do something different. Keep in mind, Jesus pulled away from his disciples and others quite frequently to commune with his Heavenly Father. This is the greatest example we have to live by, especially when are engaging in the healing process. Sometimes you have to pull away from your family and others to gain insight that may not be available or accepted by them. For example, many families in the Black community do not believe in or will not seek help because it is still the equivalent to "airing dirty laundry to strangers." This learned behavior and attitude is derived from shame that also accompanies family secrets, spanning generation after generation. Stone (2004) grappled with this phenomenon in the following:

> If abuse occurs in a family that is already coping with its own problems, be they personal, economic, social, or legal, then the situation is further complicated because the family is focused on other priorities and communication is rare or nonexistent. As my interviews with survivors show time and time again, adults often are simply not aware of their children's needs. Typically they know something is not quite right, but they say or do nothing because of fear and denial.... We may be the epitome of the Joneses, living high on the hill, or Joe and Josephine Public, struggling to get out of the projects and off welfare. Doesn't matter. If we allow a space for our children to be vulnerable and then turn our eyes from their signs of distress, abusers can strike in our homes, under our noses.... (pp. 18, 19; containing exert from Willie Mae Anthony's *Penny's Penguin's Secret*).

I have talked about the traumatized person speaking to a trusted friend or loved one earlier in this book. Let me discuss this further in the context of differentiating one's self for your own growth and healing. I began working with a female who was in her late teens until she was in her early twenties. She sought intervention on her own and was "tired of hiding all of this (explicative)! I need somebody to talk to." I allowed her to go at it, to say whatever she wanted, hoping that she would be able to purge as I looked for reoccurring themes in her story. One of the strongest sources from which many of this young woman's "issues" radiated from was her family—"They don't like to do nothing. They're negative, lazy, ignorant…." This young woman's complaints went on for about 2 to 3 meetings before I asked one question: So what are you going to do for yourself to change your situation? Stunned, speechless and confused, she did not have a clue as to what she could do. I commended her for talking to me, which was one of the features her family did not exercise (a code of silence and secrets were their way of coping or not coping with issues), and suggested that she give some thought as to how she could change her situation. Two weeks later she returned and announced: "I'm going back to school. I'm not sure what I want to study right now, but I want to see if I can do it, make something out of myself." I later learned that she had been talking to a trusted friend, who held the proverbial mirror up in front her and said, "Do something the rest of them (family members) won't do." Obtaining higher education was her answer.

In cases of victimization and/or perpetration that repeat itself within a family, one will have to differentiate from their family-of-origin by seeking outside help, working on the issues that seem to be passed down, and deciding to do something different in their own life. One may fail to progress by using excuses such as: "I don't want them to think I'm trying to be better than they are." Oh, but that's the goal! If you see that a certain behavior, attitude or condition is not working for you, it is a reasonable goal to find something that works for you. Many times these thoughts are learned within a shame-based environment, and one would need to be exposed to something or someone different from whence they came. A person whose family had endured many instances of trauma may in turn see these behaviors as "normal," may not open their mouths to anyone. This cycle then continues from one person to the next person—from one generation to the next.

Trust is an essential part of the healing process. I believe the goal of restoring trust in others and one's self should include giving people a chance to engage you in a positive way. Wall (2004) addressed trusting others in the following:

> Trusting others means relying on others' honesty and commitment to keep their promises to you... You will know when it's safe to trust someone else when you can read and trust your own feelings and have faith in a positive future. Trust is centered on the desire to trust others and to build satisfying relationships. Insecurities about how much you should trust are planted in your experiences since birth (p. 17).

When a traumatized person is able to confide in someone other than a shame-based family member, who might tell them to be quiet like Absalom told Tamar, he or she will be able to release some of the pain as a result of a painful event in his or her life. He or she feels ashamed when they are unable to or not permitted to talk about their experiences or their feelings. He or she will eventually feel as if they do not belong or that they must hide or cover things up so they will not be seen or discovered. I have heard these sayings time and time again, but they are true: "What goes up must come down" and "What goes in has to come out." The same applies to persons in distress. Whatever the noxious event was, it will replay itself in his or her mind, causing disruptions in their lives. Let's say the traumatized person does not talk about what happened to him or her, eventually it will come out, either in their behavior (addictions, abusing others, etc.), in their health (mental, emotional, physical, and spiritual), the way they socialize (intimate/romantic relationships), or in the way they survive (employment, criminality, etc.).

Fix It Jesus

As you may be able to tell by now, I am a great proponent of "letting it out;" meaning, getting to a place where you can talk about the disturbing experiences you have endured and the emotions felt as a result of those events. A major part of this process could be developing a healthy prayer life. In my role as Youth Pastor at my church, I teach and encourage the need for developing and maintaining a healthy prayer life. I also equate this healthy prayer life to developing a new relationship with a person you really want to get to know in that "you want to spend time talking with them on the phone for hours, day after day." The same effort applies in fostering a healthy prayer life where you can talk to Jesus about what is going on the inside of you. This is strongly advised, even after you are shown who it is you can trust with your feelings in regards to your experiences.

One writer, who also advocates for speaking with

trusted individuals, said the following:

> God does not intend for you to face your heartbreak
> alone. One of the ways he helps you is through other
> people. You cannot solve this deep problem privately
> and alone. Find someone (or a group of people) you
> trust. Talk and pray with them…. This might not be
> easy. Some of your friends won't know how to
> handle the aftermath of your attack (or violation).
> They might avoid you. Or they might say things that
> make you feel even worse. Ask God to help you
> forgive your friends if they say foolish things or act in
> ways that are uncaring or hurtful. Offer them the
> same forgiveness and mercy you have received from
> God… Wise friends will love you well, hang in there
> with you, point you to Jesus, and talk to you candidly
> and tenderly. If you don't have friends like this, ask
> God to provide them for you. And then look for a
> church community where you can get connected
> (Powlison, 2010, p. 27 – 28).

That sums up my whole point of the "trusted friend."
Just because one might not have a spouse or a mate does not
mean he or she is alone. God blesses us with family and
community to reach out to in troubling times. And, yes,
sometimes they do not know how to handle what you are
dealing with, but sometimes you do not know either. The key
is to find a way to forgive them and yourself. This is also
where your prayer life comes in very handy.

I Wish There Was an Easier Way

One of the most painfully difficult tasks an emotionally injured person must involve themselves in as he or she journey toward healing is learning to trust again. I know this because there are times I struggle with trusting others, even some twenty years later. However, as I have tried to explain to my younger brother, trust issues can develop over long periods of time or one to two acts of betrayal. My trust issues are the result of me repeatedly trusting others and being let down or betrayed in some way or another. Yet I found that learning how to trust Jesus taught me how to trust others. My opinion is that this can be achieved during and throughout your prayer life. In this time and space, as you talk with and listen to Jesus, you learn how to be patient to hear from others.

One of my ongoing struggles is dealing with disloyalty and treachery. I have to continuously remind myself that people are people and they are prone to making mistakes, just as I am. But what angers me is, real talk now, is when ulterior motives are concealed so well that when they do come to light, accountability goes out the window in that the other party refuses to say they had them to begin with. That makes my blood boil. I can truly appreciate being told what is sought, even if I do not like or agree with them. This shows consideration in that I can make an informed, intelligent decision as to whether I am willing to do or participate in what the other party wants to do or not. I cannot stand being lied to or conned. This is a blatant sign of disrespect and a degradation of my intelligence. I will admit this behavior may be carried out a few times before I catch on, but once

179

my patience is gone, when my Liberian scales are tipped, it usually is not a good thing for the other person because trust is not regained or earned. That relationship usually dissolves.

It is easy for others to say, "Trust me." It is a statement that is interpreted differently for those who have had their trust broken. It is terribly difficult for those whom had not learned how to trust as children. In fact, Wall (2004) wrote the following regarding the foundation of trust:

> Few people receive a solid base of trust as children. Even fewer are taught how to trust themselves. Regardless of the lessons we each received, we only learned *about* trust as children. We need to learn *how* to trust as adults... Trust is more than a mental state or feeling we can't control. Trust is a skill to be learned and a choice to be made. It is a gift to be shared with those who appreciate its importance... Trust is also fragile and must be handled with great care. Care-less words and impulsive actions can easily damage trust. Some decide early in life to seldom trust anyone, hiding their authentic self away from any possibility of rejection or betrayal. This is a safe but limited path.... ...one of learning how to trust wisely. Wisdom comes from taking the risk to reach out and trust others, while you know that you are likely to make some mistakes. This is where courage comes into play. Once you accept that you can learn from your mistakes, you'll find that trust in yourself will begin to grow (p. 5).

It is usually not a good thing to rub against or betray with a person who struggles with trust issues in that there are certain triggers (situations, conditions or behaviors) that causes him or her to digress to a place that may not be healthy for either party. In this place, he or she may exhibit behaviors that may not be favorable in a way that shows him or her in a favorable light. A person who is usually easy-going may become aggressive in ways they might not have been before. Not good!

The Wonder of Counsel

Trust is critical in the relationship you have with your therapist or counselor, if you choose to enter into this type of relationship. And like any other relationship in your life, trust has to be earned and maintained. There are higher standards and expectations within the affiliation with your therapist or counselor, as it should be. The therapist or counselor is expected to uphold certain values that the person may not have in their personal relationships with their family and friends. There has to be boundaries in place to avoid conflicts and complications within the therapeutic process.

Developing healthy boundaries within the therapeutic relationship is an integral part of the development of and preservation of trust. In fact, clear boundaries are important in every relationship in that both parties understand their role in one another's life at any given time. There are times when I serve as my younger brother's Youth Pastor while still being his brother, for example. These are two very different functions, but we both understand the context in which these roles are played out. In a therapeutic relationship, however, it must be clear-cut: the therapist or counselor is the helper and the counselee is to be helped. No other role should be held at the same time because *it will* hinder the therapeutic process. A great example of this hindrance can be seen in the relationship I had with one of my mentees—the one who struggled during the journaling process. The problem was, as I deduced after the fact, we had too many functions present at the same time and the boundaries became blurred; therefore, the journaling process grounded to a halt. Our relationship was affected as well in that I had to pull back and re-evaluate where I fit into her life. I had to decide on which role that was more important, and then, remain there in order to stay within the boundaries of that role in order to keep down confusion and/or hard feelings.

The outcome, the healing of the relationship between my mentee and me, was that we addressed the "big, pink elephant" in the middle of our relationship—the multi-layers present in our relationship. We both agreed that we were not able to deal with the many things going on and we were not able to separate all of those layers. We had to come to a place where we had to acknowledge those things, and then, work toward bonding, identifying the problem areas, and working together in order to move forward in a productive direction. This was not only accomplished through non-combative, gentle confrontation, but most importantly, prayer. I had to check my own feelings in the way I engaged my mentee, and this was an incredibly difficult undertaking. I will talk more about the need for self-evaluation later in this chapter.

What I have learned so far about boundaries is that

many boundaries, according to the relationship or affiliation, may have to be more rigid than others. However, no relational boundaries should be too loose, especially with those whom have been traumatized in the past. People who have been abused or mistreated in the past can be emotionally difficult and taxing for others to be in a meaningful relationship with them. If the boundaries are not clear from the beginning, then the relationship will suffer in some way because the lines will be crossed. Without clearly defined boundaries people tend to step into areas of your life that they really should not be in but were unaware they were not supposed be there in the first place. Therefore, some parameters or descriptions of your role within the relationship or affiliation must be understood by all parties in order to avoid "challenges" later on down the road. I observed one of my friend's relationships with a young woman for whom he served as "a trusted friend." Before long, this young woman became a member of a number of his circles and activities—"Almost to the point where she was always around." At first my friend did not seem to mind because this gave her "something to do besides wallowing in her problems." But it became problematic, however, when he noticed that they held conversations about her situation continuously in various settings—"It got to the point where I couldn't mingle without her being by my side." Overlapping or blurred boundaries!

Another painful aspect of overlapping or blurred boundaries is that they can cause trouble in many ways and to a number of people. It is interesting that distorted boundaries be included in this section because when you think about all of the things you could avoid, undue pain to others is a big one. A situation arose with an associate of mine. It seemed as if things "were crumbling all apart" in this person's life. A woman became a confidant to a person she thought she knew well enough to be that type of friend. The man appeared to be easy-going and kind-hearted, but what the woman did not know is he had a darker, manipulative side to him. The man's rationale for him asking the woman to function in that role originated from him wanting "bounce some things off of you." They became friends and began introducing one another to their friends and associates; by the way, there is nothing wrong with networking. Soon this confidant relationship became social in that they intermingled with one another's friends beyond business and networking. It came to a point where the woman's business and personal affairs took up most of her time and she was not as accessible to this guy as she once. She explained that it would be temporary and that she would be "out-and-about" again "once this storm passes." The man reluctantly said he understood and "would text her every-now-and-then," which was reasonable, especially when a person is going through something in the life.

Well, things became more convoluted as the days and weeks passed. The man, who I have already said was manipulative, launched a vicious campaign against the woman without her knowing what was going on. The man befriended and started dating her close friend weeks before things came up in the woman's life. As she weathered the trials in her life, the woman found solace in comforting herself by spending time alone to reflect and where she felt called to go in the next phase of her life. The man started feeling slighted and began dodging and avoiding the woman's friend, who told him that their mutual friend would be fine, "She does that from time-to-time in order to maintain her sanity," explained. Again, the man said, "I can understand

184

that." Yet his actions became mean and cruel towards the woman he was dating. He would brush her off, make promises he did not intend to keep, and other things he knew would hurt both women.

One of my friends/colleagues and I talk about boundaries often because "it could get dangerous with all of those layers and boundaries crossing all over the place." In other words, you really do not know whom you are dealing with until the pressure is on and the other person feel trapped or as if they have nothing to lose. "Hell, they will say or do anything," my friend said adamantly. I am grateful to have friends around who are not members of each layer of my life but they are still able to function in the roles they are in. "It's a control, you know," she says often. Point taken.

To say achieving healthy boundaries is an easy feat to accomplish would be misleading because both parties may genuinely like being around one another or the relationship is so easy and relaxed. It could be especially difficult for people who genuinely care about others and have a compassionate heart. This should never be the case in a therapeutic relationship because the boundaries will be impaired and complications will arise. When I say, "boundary lines are blurred," here is a great example of what I mean: a person with whom you are friendly with and only see from time-to-time shows up at your door on Thanksgiving Day, without being invited, and you still let them in. That person has no idea they have crossed the line by showing up. Or the example of my friend acting as the "trusted friend" in someone else's life and then she eventually became a member of various areas and activities in his life. Boundaries usually blur because one or both parties do not know they are infringing upon the other's space, personal and/or otherwise. In a therapeutic relationship, it is helpful and healthy to remember that the therapist or counselor is the helper and the counselee is being helped.

　　Some of the ways I was entangled in relationships with blurred boundaries when I decided to help friends and acquaintances. This was not good! In the first situation, the same rule applies to money—never loan money or do business with your family or friends. I thought I could maintain the lines, help an acquaintance, and keep it moving. That was good in theory but it became too complicated in that the other person's as well as my presence began to overlap into other roles and settings. We were not able to separate the various layers of our relationship. Overwhelming! In the second, I found myself understanding the other person's plight and failed to keep my eye on the ball, so to speak. Things that I would not normally tolerate took a little longer for me to recognize and react to. In one incident, it was too late for me to react so I had to make some adjustments in my mind in order maintain peace and avoid further damages of hurt feelings and broken relationships. Sometimes it is about recognizing the positions within relationships. It's not about who is above who, but about the roles held. (Epiphany!) A counselor should never have drinks with a current client because that places them in a social environment and creates a social fellowship to which the client may want to repeat—ergo, you are now friends with your client. Another case in point can be functioning in a supervisory position over a long time friend. When it is time to disagree, say no, or reprimand that person it can create problems. Or sometimes when these do not take place it can be viewed as favoritism toward your friend.

Unnecessary heartburn!

Firm boundaries are very necessary when it comes to working with people who had been violated sexually and are living with the shame of it. It is the therapist's and/or the counselor's job to be mindful of their presence and feelings while working with emotionally vulnerable people. In other words, he or she must continuously engage in self-reflection as they interact with those they work with. Some of the behaviors we need to be mindful of are: How do I engage him or her in the therapeutic setting and relationship? I know I can be flirtatious and if I am not careful I may appear to be flirting with the female I am trying to help. What happens when the person does or says something I do not like or agree with? Does it show in my body language, in my words, my facial expressions, or do I ignore them by not responding at all? How do I react when he or she lashes out at me? Do I feel the need to "set them straight"? These are but a few things we should consider repeatedly throughout the therapeutic/helping process. Our behaviors and/or reactions can make or break this process. We have to be vigilant of our boundaries, our comportment and how we relate to the other, in order not only to help the other person's health and well being, but also our sanity.

It All Fits Together

Up to this point I have mentioned some of the ways I would approach certain situations in antidotal fashion without clearly linking them to the approaches I prefer to use. I am a student of Viktor Frankl's Logotherapy. My doctoral dissertation was centered on Frankl's theory of achieving wholeness through finding meaning in one's life, and to the chagrin of some, it has become a part of my life because I am more vocal with my curiosity. Recently I have acquired a pension to study and utilize Greenberg's Emotion-Focused Therapy (EFT) approach. Combined, these two therapeutic methods will serve as the basis of my Therapeutic Pastoral Counseling ministry to those whom God sends my way.

If you recall from *No Shame in the Game*, or if this is your first time reading about Logotherapy, allow me to use this time to review and introduce it in the proceeding fashion. So what does Logotherapy mean? In a nutshell, Logotherapy is the practice of obtaining healing through meaning, or as Fabry (1988) said: "Health through meaning" (p. 1). Murasso (2008) wrote that the function of Logotherapy "seeks healing at the spiritual core of man's [humanity's] being. It is at this aspect of man [humanity] that warrants wholeness, because it is at the level of soul that man [humanity] is confronted with his [their] ontology (being)" (p. 19). Logotherapy comes from the two words: Logos, meaning *word*, and therapy, connotes *healing*. Murasso described Logos as "The Second Person of the Blessed Trinity, [and] is revealed as the Incarnate God, the Christ, to those who approach him in pursuit of healing and wholeness" (p. 15). Therefore, in many circles, Logotherapy reflects the works and ministry of Jesus.

The tenets of Logotherapy are self-discovery, choices, uniqueness, responsibility, and self-transcendence. For Frankl, these principles were tested in the German concentration camps. Frankl (1959/2006) wrote the following of himself and his fellow inmates:

The way in which a man accepts his fate and all the

188

suffering it entails, the way in which he takes up his cross, gives him ample opportunity—even under the most difficult circumstances—to add a deeper meaning to his life. It may remain brave, dignified and unselfish. Or in the bitter fight for self-preservation he may forget his human dignity and become no more than an animal. Here lies the chance for a man either to make use of or to forgo the opportunities of attaining the moral values that a difficult situation may afford him. And this decides whether he is worthy of his sufferings (p. 67).

As we continue with our discussion of Logotherapy, you will notice that it is often used when challenges come about in one's life. In many cases, there is a disruption in the flow of a person's life (i. e. loss of a job, loss of a loved one, divorce/separation, "mid-life" crisis, a decline in health, etc.). Frankl (1969/1988) spoke of suffering and pain from a Logotherapuetic stance when he said the following: "But what about inescapable suffering? Logotherapy teaches that pain must be avoided as it is possible to avoid it. But as soon as a painful fate cannot be changed, it not only must be accepted but may be transmuted into something meaningful, into an achievement" (p. 72). Regardless of the circumstances, one can find solace in connecting with his or her destiny and meaning. Frankl continued on to say, "the suffering man (person) who, by virtue of his (their) humanness, is capable of rising above, and taking a stand to, his (or her) suffering, moves in a dimension perpendicular to the former" (p. 74 – 75). In other words, a person whom is suffering can face their pain with an attitude that helps them to see their situation in a positive light—the opposite of their current position. However, it is solely dependent upon their attitude. Frankl went on to say:

A human being strives for success but, if need be, does not depend on his fate, which does or does not *allow* for success. A human being, by the very attitude he chooses, is capable of finding and fulfilling meaning in even a hopeless situation. This fact is understandable only through our dimensional approach, allots to the attitudinal values a higher dimension than to the creative and experiential values. The attitudinal values are the highest possible values (1969/1988, p. 75).

When unavoidable suffering is encountered, the person experiencing the situation will be able to place a higher value on the *meaning* of the situation when their attitude is positive and they are willing to seek the meaning behind that situation. Frankl (1959/2006) beautifully wrote about the meaning of suffering and destiny in the following manner:

"Life" does not mean something vague, but something very real and concrete, just as life's tasks are also very real and concrete. They form man's destiny, which is different and unique for each individual. No man and no destiny can be compared with any other man or any other destiny. No situation repeats itself, and each situation calls for a different response. Sometimes the situation in which a man finds himself may require him to shape his own fate by action. At other times it is more advantageous for him to make use of an opportunity for contemplation and to realize assets in this way. Sometimes many may be required simply to accept fate, to bear his cross. Every situation is distinguished by its uniqueness, and there is always only one right answer to the problem posed by the situation at hand... When a man finds that it is his destiny to suffer, he will have to accept his suffering as his task; his single and unique task. He will have to acknowledge the fact that even in suffering he is unique and alone in the universe. No one can relieve him of his suffering or suffer in his place. His unique opportunity lies in the way in which he bears his burden (p. 77).

Although these words are powerfully eloquent, they speak volumes to the uniqueness of humanity's experiences and the distinctiveness of the individual's life. It also addresses one's need to live and absorb their experiences as opportunities to grow and achieve self-transcendence, even as suffering occurs. It is very important to observe Frankl's emphasis on a person's suffering and the uniqueness of being in that place alone. An individual's suffering is meant to shape them in order to meet their destiny. In other words, distress in one's life is designed to help the individual to be prepared for their God-given work. As Frankl stated, "no one's destiny can be compared to another's." Each person's life and circumstance is different and one of a kind. Therefore, it meets the goal of Logotherapy—to help people to achieve wholeness through meaning in trying times. Frankl (1959/2006) went on to explain how he and others in the concentration camps arrived at the meaning of their suffering in the following remarks:

What was really needed was a fundamental change in our attitude toward life. We had to learn ourselves and, furthermore, we had to teach the despairing men, that *it did not really matter what we expected from life, but rather what life expected from us.* We needed to stop asking about the meaning of life, and instead to think of ourselves as those who were being questioned by life—daily and hourly, our answer must consist, not in talk and meditation, but right action and in right conduct. Life ultimately means taking the responsibility to find the right answer to its problems and to fulfill the tasks which it constantly sets for each individual (pp. 76 – 77).

Greenberg (2011) described Emotion-Focused Therapy's (EFT) features as the following:

EFT's dialectical constructivist theory of self-functioning, in which experience is symbolized and constructed into a coherent narrative… In this view, emotion helps the organism to process complex situational information rapidly and automatically, in order to produce action appropriate for meeting important basic needs (e.g., attachment, identity). Emotions provide rapid, automatic appraisals of significance of situations to people's well-being and therefore guide adaptive action… In addition, rather than viewing problems as arising only from the disregulation of emotion (i.e., being overwhelmed by them) as well as by maladaptive emotional responding based on painful feeling (e.g., fear, shame) stemming from past experience (pp. 31, 32, 33).

Going forward, EFT and Logotherapy are a wonderful fit in that EFT centers around constructing meaning through narration to the emotions we experience; while Logotherapy seeks to achieve wholeness through discovering and living out meaning in one's life. In other words, the two complement one another because their collective goals are to help us to become the people God created us to be. We were fashioned with emotions and natural reactions to environmental and internal situations, which causes us to consider what is occurring and how it affects our functioning. Therefore, a centralized mechanism within our emotional core is necessary in our continuous quest to give meaning to what is going on around and within us. Fabry (1987) astutely asserted:

> ...all reality has meaning (logos) and that life never ceases to have meaning for anyone; that meaning is very specific and changes from person to person and for unique and each life contains a series of unique demands that have to be discovered and responded to, that the response to these provides meaning; and that happiness, contentment, peace of mind, and self-actualization are mere side products in the search for meaning (p. 9).

Connotations

Now that we have an understanding of the meaning of Logotherapy and Emotion-Focused Therapy, let's see how they can be applied to a situation to which a person can benefit emotionally. Do you recall the two examples—"a throw away" and "nobody really wants me"—that was shown earlier in this chapter? I want to use them to show how Logotherapy and EFT can be applied in a beneficial way. Although I stated that the young man who felt like "a throw away" reached an epiphany wherein he was able to acknowledge he was loved and created to be and do ("God didn't make me to be like them, God wants me to do something...."), he did not get there overnight. Several events transpired during the period of time that we talked. He still had to interact with the same people he felt used and discarded him once they took what they wanted from him. In his pursuit to be loved for who he was and not for what he could do, this young desperately tried to win favor "without doing" things he really did not want to do.

Each time the young man experienced something disturbing during the time he spent with those whom he felt should have loved and cared for him, I would help him to probe into what he felt and assign a feeling to it. In other words, I would talk him through what happened, the results, and what he thought and endured. It was tempting to say to him, "Stay away from them;" but the people in question were significant to him. This provided a solid place to start probing and processing his triggers and how they affect his judgment as he decides to be around those who use and hurt him repeatedly. After some prodding and encouragement, various themes emerged. This young man, who endured so many bouts of abandonment and rejection, so desperately wanted them to "accept me for who I am," that he failed to acknowledge what he felt whenever he was invited to join his current significant others. In other words, he chose to ignore what his gut (we call this "the unction of the Holy Spirit") and go anyway. What was even more saddening about this is this young man said, "I knew they mighta been up to something, but…"

The example of the young woman who believed "nobody really wants me" is a great example of how Logotherapy can be beneficial in the therapeutic setting. To be clearer as to how this young woman caught the eye of the other woman, I will give more information regarding the way the younger woman presented herself to the world. To those who encountered and observed this young woman, she appeared to be "promiscuous" and "lose" in that she dressed provocatively and "was not lady-like" in the way that she interacted with others. In fact, some people preferred that their children not be around her at times. As the older woman continued to spend time with and was making an impact on the younger woman's life, the former beginning to address some areas that the former was not prepared to acknowledge (i. e., the way she dressed and behaved around the opposite sex). The older woman discovered dressed and carried herself the same way that the older women in her family did. To her, "It doesn't mean anything," because she was so accustomed to these things.

Unfortunately, this type of scenario plays itself out in many different ways and with both genders; and with those who are of impressionable ages as well as adults, who should "know better." When people do not understanding their meaning, their significance in life, they are bound to listlessly follow the dictates of the "crowd." In Frankl's *Man's Search for Ultimate Meaning* (2000), he described his treatment of self-discovery, or the will to meaning, and how it plays a crucial role in one's journey towards self-transcendence in that it "denotes the fundamental fact that normally man [people] is striving to find, and fulfill, meaning and purpose in life" (p. 85). In other words, people try hard to make sense of their lives when faced with situations that challenge what they believe. When the older woman questioned the younger woman, the latter probably felt that the former was "judging her," rather than stretching her to find meaning in her life, to discover who God intended for her to be.

Assigning descriptive words to how one feels during

and/or following an unpleasant event can be a tedious task in that one feels as if they have to relive or rehash what happened to them again. However, within this portion of the therapeutic exchange to phases of Greenberg's (2011, p. 82 - 83) "Phases of Treatment" can be achieved over time (1. bonding and awareness, and 2. evoking and exploring). The counselor/therapist is most effective when he or she is able to connect and empathize with the person with whom they are helping. The helper must also confirm what the person says he or she might be feeling by acknowledging and respecting what is said. By doing so, the person may feel comfortable in evoking or reliving the details of the event and exploring and/or delving further into what those emotions mean to him or her. This can be groundbreaking in that he or she may discover things about themselves that may not have been acknowledged or known before this course of action. By accomplishing this feat in the person's understanding of themselves and those situations, he or she can then proceed onto altering their reactions and feelings regarding the situation they had endured (phase three, transformation).

* * * * *

Recovery and restoration following tragic events, such as sexual violations, is not only needed in an individual's life but there are many questions that may come along this journey. Let's face it: Who deserves to be violated in such a horrendous manner? A good friend of mine and I had a conversation that was along the lines of the age old nature versus nurture debate. There was a highly publicized case where a woman had been sexually assaulted and the trial was televised. As to be expected, the woman was made to be the villain by the defense attorney. Most disturbing was the fact that the attorney said she "provoked this attack by being seductively alluring." Yikes! Once the outrage passed, my friend and I meticulously processed the possible implications that this attorney's statement could have contained. We took our conversation in another direction. Instead of pontificating on how ridiculous this man's statement was or why he should have or should not have said this or that. We utilized what we understood about human development and nature versus nurture.

This entire book is about human nature and development. As we are born and develop into the people we are today, we have been equipped with certain skills and tools that enables us to function from day-to-day. Too many times we are shown things but are not taught their meanings and true usage. Therefore, when these skills and tools are used they may be utilized improperly.

As was said before, no one deserves to be sexually violated, period. Let's analyze the attorney's statement when he said the woman who was attacked had "provoked this attack by being seductively alluring" in the context of Emotion-Focused Therapy and Logotherapy for a moment. I will create a scenario of this woman's upbringing to come up with a plausible rationale for such a statement, because a lot can be ascertained for therapeutic purposes.

Linda was born in the early 1970s. She was the forth daughter of six sisters, and she grew up with both of her parents present in her home. Linda's extended family was also predominately comprised of women. Her father worked and administered some discipline to his daughters, but he was not the leading figure in this regard. Linda's mother was dominating in that her personality and parenting style ran along the dictatorship lines. Linda and her sisters were

197

exposed to their parents' siblings as well, which also happened to be comprised of mostly women. Linda had the opportunity to observe and interact with a myriad of different female personalities and how men related to them. Linda's mother taught her daughters to be strong and forward in that they "let them know what you want out of life." This was reinforced by their father and extended family members. So you can imagine what kind of household this was with so many strong personalities living under the same roof?

Linda had several aunts who were influential in her life. One in particular was her Aunt Fran, affectionately known as "Auntie Franie." Fran was strong, confident, loving, successful and outspoken. Fran repeatedly encouraged Linda to "go get what you want out of life." Linda did so in her educational and professional pursuits. There was also another side to Aunt Fran that also intrigued Linda—Auntie Franie's softer, captivating side, especially with men. Auntie Franie had a way in the way she moved, dressed, and spoke that seemed to drive the fellas crazy. Linda observed Franie's ways as a child and was said be "just like that Franie" when she entered adolescence. Linda earned the reputation of being "too free" and popular with the boys. She was not particularly sexually promiscuous, nor was she overly flirtatious. However, she did appear to be restless because she changed boyfriends on what seemed like a weekly basis. This type of behavior continued until the boys in her surroundings were reluctant to show interest in her for fear that they would develop feelings for her, and she would change her mind about them and move onto the next boy— and for what appears to be for no apparent reason. Auntie Franie, who never married, did the same in her life. What Linda learned earlier on in her life was: You gotta have a man at times, at all costs. She was never educated on the connotations/implications of her actions as a young woman. And for this, Linda's life was impacted in ways no one anticipated. In actuality, Linda had a number of insecurities she wanted to keep hidden in that many of her spoken words were not matched by her actions. She was seen as contrary because of her contradictory words and behaviors. Linda never took this observation seriously, even after she had been warned many times through the years.

From a Logotherapuetic and EFT stand point, Linda was never *TAUGHT* the possible ramifications of these actions and how they could have been perceived. She could not grasp why she had been treated so egregiously by another human being, especially by someone she knew. At some point during the trial and in her therapeutic process the emotional floodgates opened and the questions came forth to Linda's astonishment. As it turned out, she had never learned enough about herself nor did she appreciate the peace in being without a man in her life. One of the most pertinent questions Linda was asked was: How does it feel for you to being in the presence of yourself? Baffled, Linda responded by saying, "Who?" This was indicative of her lack of being comfortable in being alone without being lonely or being comfortable with herself. As the trial proceeded, Linda came to understand many painful truths about which she had come be in life.

With her therapist, Linda decided to take an aggressive approach to address her vast inner yearnings. "I've decided to take a real look at my life and my upbringing to see how I can change for myself," Linda emphatically announced. The therapist informed Linda that she intended to differentiate, "and this can be achieved by assigning meaning to many of the things you have learned in your life." Linda determined that "this dreadful event in my life would not be a hindrance" in her life, "but it will help me to become a stronger, better person."

Linda's therapeutic process entailed assertive aspects wherein the therapist slowly and compassionately helped her to verbalize the incident in question, which brought her into the therapeutic relationship. Linda was able to come to a place where she could tell the entire story without having to be encouraged, prompted or redirected by the therapist. She also arrived at a place where she no longer blamed herself for the actions of another person—the assailant. Of course, Linda thought this was all to the therapeutic process but the therapist abruptly informed her that "this is only the beginning."

The next phase was to seek and assign meaning to many aspects of Linda's life, namely meaning in her life. This proved to be most daunting for her because no one had taken the time to attend to this area of life with Linda. Linda had to make some adjustments in order to stay on track and address aspects of her life outside of the realm of her physical features. This presented another challenge because of the sexual assault she had endured. Eventually, Linda courageously embraced: "My body is not all there is to me."

Linda was able to attain the primary elements of Logotherapy and EFT in that she was able to see there was something beyond her experiences and how she felt about them. In Logotherapy, there is a profound function in suffering because it adds to one's predestined purpose in life. In other words, it was truly unfortunate that Linda was sexually violated but that was not the end of her story. She had to live after the dust settled. In EFT, there was something to acknowledging and giving meaning to the emotions felt at certain times, in certain situations. This enabled Linda to cope, adjust and navigate these areas of her life in a way that allowed her to function without too many complications. Greenberg (2011) succinctly described the goal of EFT for the person in the ensuing manner:

Clients are helped in EFT to better identify, experience, accept, explore, make sense of, transform, and flexibly manage their emotions. As a result, clients become more skillful in accessing the important information and meanings about themselves and their world that emotions provide, as well as become more skillful in using that information to live vitally and adaptively. Clients in therapy are also encouraged to face dreaded emotions in order to process and transform them. A major premise guiding intervention in EFT is that transformation is possibly only when individuals accept themselves as they are. EFT is an approach designed to help clients become aware of and make productive use of their emotions (p. 5).

The examples shared are, as simplistic as they may seem, may give you but a glimpse into how I seek to serve others. I strongly believe the combination of Logotherapy and Emotion-Focused Therapy will prove to be powerful tools for me as I go forth to serve and assist God's wounded children. I, being a wounded but not broken child of God, can really appreciate the intent of these methods in that they help us to seek, assign, explore, and, most of all, understand many things and events that occur in our lives. By no means do these methods guarantee that all of our sorrows will be understood but they can help us to live them in a more productive manner.

Epilogue:

It's about the Healing

Now that this writing process has come to an end, I would be remised not to speak on Tamar for whom this book is and my future counseling ministry will be named after. I believe her story set the tone for what I believe God is leading me to carry out in my life's work and ministry—caring and sharing with others in a way that will allow them to be freed from their traumatic experiences. That was the goal of this book. In Tamar's situation, so many people who were charged to care for and protect her victimized her. All she needed, even before being raped, was someone to love on her in a way that she deserved to be loved. From all appearances, Tamar did not have the support and the nurturance she needed to be able to stand against the enemy's actions. Instead she was left out there to fend for herself. She tried to stop Amnon from committing an atrocious act, she tried to connect with Absalom, and she wanted her father, King David, to do something about it; but none of these things happened. Tamar, in many senses, was an emotionally abandoned orphan. That is how she easily came to live out the rest of her life in desolation.

In today's American society, there are far too many people suffering by the hands of those whom are supposed to love and protect them. But God has a plan for their lives. Tragic situations are robbing people of hope and confidence in a world that our loving God has created, leaving many to ask why and how these things could have happened the way they did. I truly believe these things can be used for the up building of God's kingdom if God is allowed to be a part of the healing process.

The "rugged individualism" mentality has certainly

202

tainted our view of this world. "Survival of the fittest" seems to be the mantra and it seems like people just do not care for one another the way they should. Even if one tries to care for others it is met with suspicion—"What does he or she want in return?" This is absolutely wrong and I do not believe this is what God would have us to do. The Bible clearly stated in Galatians 6:

> Dear friends, if a Christian (or person) is overcome by some sin, you who are godly should gently and humbly help that person back onto the right path. And be careful not to fall into the same temptation yourself. Share each other's troubles and problems, and in this way obey the law of Christ. If you think you are too important to help someone in need, you are only fooling yourself. You are really a nobody. Be sure to do what you should, for then you will enjoy the personal satisfaction of having done your work well, and you won't need to compare yourself to anyone else. For we are responsible for our own conduct (vv. 1 – 5, *NLT*).

This ought to be all of humanity's focus: To help someone else. I do see how this may seem a bit corny or wishfully thinking, but can you imagine what kind of world this would be if more compassion was shown? I understand the reality does not always match the utopia of a worldwide beloved community that Reverend Doctor Martin L. King, Jr. spoke of some years ago. However, I do believe this vision should continue to be held as the standard, for this is where Tamar's Healing resides—in the arms of Jesus.

About the Author

Reverend Doctor Kasim Ali Sidney Jones was born on October 11, 1971 to Reverend Shirley A. Jones Bryant and the late Curtis B. Calloway in Belleville, New Jersey. He grew up in East Orange, N. J., where he was the youngest of four boys. In 1990, he became the proud "big brother" of Tihira S. Jones-Anderson, and Roy and Connie Anderson followed thereafter. Dr. Jones received his primary and secondary education in the East Orange School System and he graduated from East Orange High School in June of 1991. He attended Essex County College and transferred to Kean University (formerly Kean College), where he earned a Bachelor of Social Work degree in 1999. Dr. Jones relocated to Atlanta, Georgia in the summer of 1999, where he studied at the Interdenominational Theological Center, and earned a Master of Divinity degree in Pastoral Care and Counseling with a dual concentration in Psychology of Religion and Sociology of Relgion. Finally, Dr. Jones studied at Argosy University in Sarasota, Florida, where he earned a Doctorate of Education in Pastoral Community Counseling.

Dr. Jones has worked with and advocated for youths for over 20 years. Since his teens, Dr. Jones has been a confidant to a number of his peers as they struggled with family and personal issues. Dr. Jones volunteered at various agencies and shelters in the East Orange and Newark, N. J. area throughout the 1990s. He mentored several teens during his career whom have reached adulthood and pursued their dreams in various ways. Dr. Jones is a firm believer in the example of Jesus Christ, when he reached out to others and helped them to see and pursue their purpose for their lives.

Dr. Jones continued to pursue his passion educationally by earning a BSW, and begun his career by working with young adults with emotional and psychological challenges. In the spring of 1999, Dr. Jones acknowledged his calling into the Counseling Ministry. He began studying Pastoral Counseling at the Interdenominational Theological Center (the ITC) in August of that same year. He began attending the Chapel of Christian Love Baptist, under the leadership of Reverend Doctor James Allen Milner, Sr., soon after arriving in Atlanta, and began working in the Youth Department to which he later became the Youth Pastor. Dr. Jones also worked in various secular capacities where he was able to contribute to the well being of children/youth and their families. Currently, Dr. Jones is a Board Certified Christian Counselor and Therapist (GA), Clinician/Therapist, and an Associate Pastor (Chapel of Christian Love Baptist, Atlanta, GA). Dr. Jones is the Dean of the College at American Bible University. He is very happy and willing to serve the Lord in these capacities.

References

Allen, D. F. (2010). *Shame: The human nemesis.* Washington, D. C.: Eleuthera Publications.

Allender, D. B. (2008). *The wounded heart: Hope for adult victims of childhood sexual abuse,* revised edition. Colorado Springs, CO: Navpress.

American Psychiatric Association (2013). *Desk reference to the diagnostic criteria DSM-5* (Diagnostic and Statistical Manual of Mental Disorders). Washington, D. C.: American Psychiatric Publications.

Boyd-Franklin, N. (1989). Black families in therapy: A multisystems approach. New York: The Guilford press.

Bradshaw, J. (1995). *Family Secrets: The path from shame to healing.* New York: Bantam Books.

_____ (2005). *Healing the shame that binds you,* expanded and updated edition. Deerfield Beach, Fl: Health Communications, Inc.

Branson, B. and P. J. Silva (2007). *Violence among us: Ministry to families in crisis.* Valley Forge: Judson Press.

Collins, G. R. (2001). *Christian Coaching: Helping others turn potential in reality.* Colorado Springs, CO: NavPress.

Dayton, T. (1997). *Heartwounds: The impact of unresolved trauma and grief on relationships.* Deerfield Beach, Fl: Health Communications, Inc.

DeGruy, J. (2005). *Post traumatic slave syndrome: America's legacy of enduring injury and healing.* Portland, OR: Joy DeGruy Publications, Inc.

Diederich, F. R. (2006/2012). *Healing the hurts of your past: A guide to overcoming the pain of shame.* Cross Point Publishing.

Engel, B. (2006). *Healing your emotional self: A powerful program to help you raise your self-esteem, quiet your inner critic, and overcome your shame.* Hoboken, N. J.: John Wiley & Sons, Inc.

Fabry, J. B. (1988). *Guideposts to meaning: Discovering what really matters.* Oakland, CA: New Harbinger Publications.

Frankl, V. E. (1959/2006). *Man's search for meaning.* Boston: Beacon Press.

_____ (1959/2006). *Man's search for meaning.* Boston: Beacon Press.

Goffman, E. (1963). *Stigma: Notes on the management of spoiled identity.* New York, N. Y.: A Touchstone Book.

Greenberg, L. S. (2011). *Emotion-focused therapy.* Washington, D. C.: American Psychological Association.

Grier, W. H. and P. M. Cobbs (2000). *Black Rage.* Eugene, OR: Wipf and Stock Publishers.

Holcomb, J. S. & L. A. Holcomb (2011). Rid of my disgrace: Hope and healing for victims of sexual assault. Wheaton, Il: Crossway.

hooks, b. (2003). *Rock my soul: Black people and self-esteem.* New York: Atria Books.

Jamal, M. (2011). When girls don't tell: Survivor's story about child sexual abuse and revictimization.

Kaufman, G. (1992). *Shame: The power of caring*, third edition, revised and expanded. Rochester, Vermont: Schenkman Books, Inc.

_____ (1996). *The psychology of shame: Theory and treatment of shame-based syndromes*, second edition. New York, N. Y.: Springer Publishing Company.

Kaufman, G. & L. Raphael (1991). *Dynamics of power: Fighting shame & building self-esteem*, revised edition.

Lewis, M. (1995). *Shame: The exposed self.* New York, N. Y.: The Free Press.

Loftus, E. & K. Ketcham (1994). *The myth of repressed memory: False memories and allegations of sexual abuse.* New York: St. Martin's Griffin.

Malone, H. (2006). *Shame: Identity theft.* Irving, TX: Vision Life Publications.

Maltz, W. (2012). *The sexual healing journey: A guide for survivors of sexual abuse*, third edition. New York: William Morrow.

Matsakis, A. (1998). *Trust after trauma: A Guide to relationships for survivors and those who love them.* Oakland, CA: New Harbinger Publications, Inc.

Merrian-Webster dictionary and thesaurus (2007). Springfield, Massachusetts: Merrian-Webster, Incorporated.

Murasso, J. N. (2008). *Logotherapy and the logos of God in Christic wisdom.* Belleville, Ontario, Canada: Guardian Books.

Powlison, D. (2010). *Sexual assault: Healing steps for victims.* Greensboro, N. C.: New Growth Press.

Ramsland, K. and P. N. McGrain (2010). *Inside the minds of sexual predators.* Santa Barbara, CA: Praeger.

Seasmands, D. A. (1991). *Healing for damaged emotions: Recovering from the memories that cause our pain.* Colorado Springs, CO: Chariot Victor Publishing.

Smedes, L. B. (1993). *Shame & grace: Healing the shame we don't deserve.* New York, N. Y.: Zondervan Publishing House.

Sorensen, M. J. (2006). *Breaking the chains of low self-esteem,* second edition. Sherwood, OR: Wolf Publishing Company.

Stone, R. D. (2004). *No secrets no lies: How Black families can heal from sexual abuse.* New York: Harlem Moon Broadway Books.

Townsend, J. (2011). Beyond boundaries: Learning to trust again in relationships. Grand Rapids, MI: Zondervan.

Tracy, S. R. (2005). *Mending the soul: Understanding and healing abuse.* Grand Rapids, Michigan: Zondervan.

Wall, C. L. (2004). *The courage to trust: A guide to building deep and lasting relationships.* Oakland, CA: New Harbinger Publications, Inc.

Warren, R. (2002). *The Purpose Driven Life: What on Earth Am I here for?* Zondervan: Grand Rapids.

Welch, E. T. (2012). *Shame interrupted: How God lifts the pain of worthlessness and rejection.* Greensboro, NC: New Growth Press.

Wilson, S. D. (1990). *Released from shame: Recovery for adult children of dysfunctional families.* Downers Grove, IL: Intervarsity Press.

Wimberly, E. P. (1999). *Moving From shame to Self-Worth: Preaching & Pastoral Care.* Nashville: Abingdon Press.

Woodley, J. (2013). *A wildflower grows in Brooklyn: From striving to thriving after sexual abuse and other trauma.* Eugene, Oregon: Resource Publications.